I0434325

The Music in Your Brother's Name

Christian James Vanderveen

March 23, 1990—April 12, 1993

The Music in Your Brother's Name

An Open Letter To My Surviving Children

Vicki W. Vanderveen

Writers Club Press
San Jose New York Lincoln Shanghai

The Music in Your Brother's Name
An Open Letter To My Surviving Children

All Rights Reserved © 2001 by Vicki W. Vanderveen

No part of this book may be reproduced or transmitted in any form or by any means, graphic, electronic, or mechanical, including photocopying, recording, taping, or by any information storage retrieval system, without the permission in writing from the publisher.

Writers Club Press
an imprint of iUniverse.com, Inc.

For information address:
iUniverse.com, Inc.
5220 S 16th, Ste. 200
Lincoln, NE 68512
www.iuniverse.com

ISBN: 0-595-16379-3

Printed in the United States of America

To You, the Reader

I am sorry you have picked up this book. It means that you are grieving—perhaps a child, perhaps a sibling—or the child of someone close to you. You have my deepest sympathy. Unfortunately, I know your pain, too well.

I am, at once, grateful and sorry for the friends who were there to help my husband, Larry, and I heal, following the death of our precious son, Christian James. They listened when we grieved out loud, and comforted when we grieved in silence. They missed work to be near, they stayed up late consoling, they drove hours to be with us, they brought food—they did for us all that we could not think to do ourselves. And most amazing of all, they did it while grieving themselves. You will never know how valuable you have been to us: Lisa, Rick, Lorraine, Scott, Aunt Judy, Linda, Robb, Laurie, Kat, Pam, and, last but not least, Bridey. They were with us through it all. There are others whose deeds are too many to list, but my thanks to them as well.

To the grandparents and great-grandparents who survived Christian—Jo (Mom), Jim (Dad), Joe, Jerry, Wilma, Grandma Slatton, Granny Bee, OerPake Snits and OerBeppe Stiens—and to the countless aunts, uncles, and cousins who barely had a chance to know my boy, my gratitude and my condolences.

This book is inspired by Christian James Vanderveen, our firstborn child. It was written, with love, for Anneka Wynne, Katrina Griet, Liesel Karinna, and Annelies Katrin Vanderveen, our surviving daughters. It was encouraged by my best friend and husband—my lifeline and anchor—Larry, whose soul is the only one in the universe that can fully know my grief.

But it is dedicated to grieving parents everywhere, that they may know they are not alone.

EPIGRAPH

" 'Tis better to have loved and lost than never to have loved at all."
Alfred Tennyson

CONTENTS

To Anneka, Katrina, Liesel and, of course, Annelies,

My dear, sweet daughters, there are lessons in life that are so painful—so horrifying to learn—if I could save you from learning them I would. But God has an agenda, and we all have lessons to learn—most good, some bad, a few intolerable. So I will try to be as eloquent here as possible, and just maybe, if I can put into words what grief is, you will learn the harshest of these from me and never have to experience it firsthand. That is a mother's duty—at least, to try.

I am not an expert in grief. I did not set out to make it my life's work. I am, however, a parent who has lost a child and a child who has lost a parent. From infancy, we dread losing a parent. But we *dread* it—it is practically inevitable. Sad truth that it is, that is the natural course of life. The alternative to losing a parent is that they will bury a child. It is *unnatural* to lose a child.

So it is your brother's death that I base this letter. These observations are mine and mine alone. Much of this may be painful for you to know. I make no apologies for my words—politically incorrect or brutal that they may be. This letter is for you, my girls, so that you may benefit from my observations and my pain.

There are things you must learn. They are not written in some textbook somewhere. I know—because I have read the books looking for answers.

There were none to be found. So here, my children, I give to you the wisdom of the lessons I have learned, because only someone who has lost a child can teach them.

Let me tell you about your brother's death. Not as I tell you now—a mother to a child—but as you someday will be able to understand it, God willing, from one adult to another. You see, grief is not necessarily a bad thing, and I want you to know that. Oh, I am not going to sugarcoat it, but there is an appreciation for life that comes only after you realize how tender and precious life is. Someday, you may wake up after the bleakest night of your life, and there will be a spectacular sunrise, meant only for you, and you will understand what I am trying to say.

I honestly believe, without hesitation, that I am the luckiest woman alive—in spite of having lost a child. If God was going to send Christian James to Earth for only three years and twenty days, I am so grateful he let ME have him. And my blessings didn't end there. I was blessed four more times with you girls. And right alongside me was your father. What a kind and generous God to reward me so!

You will hear in your lifetime, people say it is the worst tragedy in the world to lose a child. They are wrong. It would have been far sadder had I never had the opportunity to know your brother—and sadder still, I would not have known what my life was missing.

CHRISTIAN

Dear Christian, Son of Mine,

> *So now you're gone?*
> *And we're left*
> *in the empty house*
> *where you played*
> *and took your first steps*
> *and ate your meals*
> *and rode the dog.*
>
> *With you gone,*
> *the house is much bigger*
> *the dining room table is immense*
> *the TV is too loud*
> *and my work is cut in half.*
>
> *Let me tell you*
> *about the dreadful first hours*
> *after you died*
> *Because, you see,*
> *I can still smell your vomit*
> *in the blankets*
> *but they've been washed*
> *and for days I could*
> *taste your orange Jell-O*

on my lips
where you threw up
after I brought you back
with CPR
and my fingertip still
throbs
when I think of how you bit me
in your last moments
with wild eyes
pleading
or maybe
saying goodbye.

A shroud
was lifted
from my shoulders
when the
Medical Examiner
absolved me
of blame
and gave
your death
a name
and put to rest
images of a Bosnian baby
I didn't know
with sunken eyes
so deep
you looked like a skull
and head so swollen
I couldn't recognize
my own child

laying on the couch
and skin so cold
that when you were
pronounced dead
you were just as warm
and looked better.

You never bought ice cream
from a truck
or flew a kite
or pitched a no-hitter
or went skydiving
But
you did
see Big Bird in person
and chased geese
and made a bird-feeder
out of peanut butter and a pinecone
and finally got your
Cozy Coupe
Because,
like your Dad,
the car is everything.

At first,
your father
and I
clung to each other
reveling in
the other's memories,
But now
we grieve

independently
because
neither one of us
can be strong
for the other one
anymore.

But, Sunshine,
know that we will be OK.
You've brought us
closer to God
in more than
one way
and your father and I
who have shared
so much in the past
now have your
death to share, too,
and we can remember
you
to our next children
and tell them of the
brother
they never knew
and take them
to visit the grave
of a boy who never
reached forty inches tall
and write poems
in your honor
and blow
"kisses to Christian" in the air.

When I get down
I relive my memories of
how you
hosted peanut butter parties
for your playmates
and brought out a jar and six spoons
and how you tried to teach your doll
to walk
while I taught your sister
and how you would
listen to stories
for as long as anyone was willing
to read
and how you smelled,
sometimes, of maple syrup and ketchup
at the same time.

Tell me,
what lessons
did I teach you
so successfully in
three years
that God sent
you here to learn from me
so that I may
NOT teach your brothers and sisters
them until I am
ready to die
even though
maybe we both
always knew

you would die young—
so much foreshadowing—
and your death
was what I've been
preparing for my whole life.

Like the moment
of your conception
I knew the moment
you died
even though
the death certificate
says forty minutes later
(but it reads the wrong
birth-date, too).
A shudder went through
my body
and so much happened
in that split-second
and it wasn't
all bad
and I knew you
were OK
and I would be, too.

I love you,
         Mom

VWV May 26, 1993

I have to admit: it was as close to a storybook life as you could get. High school sweethearts, your father, Larry, and I married just weeks after our college graduation. A few years later, a house, then a puppy, then a son, then a daughter followed. Everything seemed to fall into place in the order it was supposed to. And if I had been the architect, I could not have designed more beautiful children for myself—any of you. It was how I had always imagined my life would turn out, I suppose. Sure, we had problems. But in retrospect, they were not as monumental as I believed them to be. Rarely, are they.

I *knew* I was blessed—or maybe just blissfully naïve. Even as a small child, I have always known I was one of God's favorites—an arrogant certainty that has always allowed me a feeling of security.

I will start on April 9, 1993, Good Friday, because sometimes I forget you don't know all the details of your brother's death. Your father came home early that day, beating the Easter weekend traffic. The weather was sunny and warm—a welcome change from the frigid New England winter. It even felt like the perfect day. I can not explain the rapture that day. In retrospect, I suppose, it was God's grace.

After a quick meal at a fast food place, we headed for the carnival. An elderly woman at the restaurant stopped me as we were leaving; she looked deeply into my eyes and pronounced, "You have a beautiful family. Cherish them." *Words to live by.*

Three-year old Christian had never been to a carnival before. If I had known it would have been the last healthy day of his life, I would never have brought him home from there; he relished every moment of it. Your father and I absorbed the carnival with renewed youth, through your brother's eyes—with its brightly lit midway and colorful rides, the aromas, the games, the sounds, all of it. I can still hear Christian's laughter when he rode the helicopter-ride.

Maybe he picked up a bug there that night, I don't know. But the next morning when we awoke, Christian was already up, playing in the living room—highly unusual, since he never got up without waking us. *Was it a bellyache that woke him early? Did he realize he only had a few more precious hours on Earth, and chose to make the most of each one? Had he been up for a while, reliving the perfect evening before?* I will never have all the answers.

I made a big breakfast of blueberry pancakes. But right after breakfast, Christian got sick to his stomach. He had never vomited before, so we had to show him how to bend over. At first, he went right back to playing, so we figured it was just something he ate. But as the day wore on, he was having a harder time keeping anything down. By nightfall, he was vomiting every twenty minutes, like clockwork. Our traditional Easter-eve egg dyeing consisted of tossing the hardboiled eggs into cups, just to get it done. And there would be no egg-hunt on Easter morn, either.

But Easter morning, Christian was very concerned about what the bunny had left for him. His basket remained largely untouched, save for the "Capt. Picard Star Trek" action figure he received. He held on to the doll most of the day. And he wanted to know why year-old sister Anneka didn't get a "Star Cake" doll, too. [Watching "Star Trek: Next Generation" was a Sunday night ritual, in our house, with Christian perched on your father's lap. One of the many things we missed, after he was gone.]

The doctor prescribed an anti-nausea medicine for him that morning. It seemed to help. He was even well enough to go for a quick trip to the store with your father. But in the afternoon, we had a hard time waking him from his nap. Your grandparents, Pake and Beppe, had come up for a quiet Easter dinner. Beppe gave Christian a stuffed bunny, which he clutched throughout dinner.

"Make it better, Daddy," he would plead, while rubbing his tummy. But Daddy couldn't—no one could.

That evening, we camped out at the Emergency Room, for several hours. Something was wrong; I could sense it, but not articulate it. But, the hospital personnel only saw a boy with the flu, and he was de-prioritized, without ever having any of his vital signs checked. Hour after hour, we watched as every case that came through the door was given precedence over the boy who was quietly dying in our arms. Finally, frustrated and tired, we left, having never seen a doctor that night.

The next morning Christian seemed somewhat better. He asked for ice cream for breakfast. He had more energy than he had for two days, but still he wasn't quite himself.

Early that morning (Monday), our family doctor called to check on Christian, having heard nothing from the ER the night before. "Bring him to my office anyway. I want to see for myself." So, to the doctor's office we trudged—Anneka, Christian, and me.

"He's got the flu—like every other kid I've seen this week. Don't let him get dehydrated. Keep doing what you're doing. Call me if anything changes," he said.

Christian walked out of the doctor's office on his own two feet. Four hours later he was dead.

The morning after his death, the medical examiner announced that Christian had died of Reye Syndrome, a rare disorder often associated with aspirin or aspirin-containing products—even though he had never had aspirin. But four years later, the same doctor who had seen Christian the morning he died, discovered the possibility that the Reye Syndrome was, in fact, an inherited metabolic disorder. [Metabolic disorders, as we would eventually find out, sometimes masquerade as Reye Syndrome, attacking the liver and brain the same way.] Essentially, Christian starved to death, right before my eyes, in a matter of hours, following a run-of-the-mill case of the flu.

Because it is a genetic condition, you girls were at risk of also having it. All of you were tested, at the doctor's insistence. Liesel tested positive for *methylmalonic acidemia* (MMA)—the likely cause of your brother's death.

To be honest, your father and I were somewhat reluctant to have you tested. We were certain it would be negative. I can't say we were ever one-hundred percent comfortable with the medical examiner's post-mortem diagnosis, but it was a nice, neat explanation and put a close to his death. Having you girls tested was like reopening his grave. Emotionally, it was almost as stressful as Christian's death.

I can't speak for the doctor, but I have often thought that his discovery of Liesel's MMA, in some way, lightened his conscience regarding his role in Christian's death. I am reluctant to use the word *redeemed,* because I don't hold him responsible for the death.

I hold no malice against the doctor—he gave Christian a thorough exam and he explained in detail what he was looking for and what he found. Most importantly, the doctor is only human; he can not see everything, and ultimately, it was God who chose to take my son.

GRIEF

This grief of mine,
I wear it like a shroud,
Around my shoulders,
I take comfort in its warmth.
I feel secure in it.
I covet it narcissistically,
I adore it selfishly.
It is my own.
And when another
Generously offers to lift it from my shoulders
I politely decline:
> *"No, thank you. I'll keep it a while longer."*
I hug it to my bosom,
In place of the child
Whose place it took.

I am not anxious to give it up,
This grief of mine,
Despite its weight and
The burden of carrying it.

I brazenly wear it—
Like Joseph with his own Coat of Many Colors
Amidst whispers
From those who do not understand

My sense of style,
My grief.
Its hood and cloak,
They envelop me.
I would gladly give it up
And stand naked and cold
To have back the child whose place it took.
But since I can't—
I snuggle deeper into its now downy familiarity.

This grief of mine, I wear it like a shroud.

VWV April 13, 1994 (Easter)

You asked me what grief was, with your child-like curiosity. (Little did you realize how well you already know it.) And this is what I told you, "It is a sadness so great they had to invent a new word just to describe how much you hurt."

But it is more than that.

Grief is a selfish emotion. It was new to me. I had never really grieved, before losing Christian. Oh, I thought I had—break-ups with boyfriends, a distant grandfather's death, even the many times we relocated because of your grandfather's military career. But only after your brother died, did I realize I could hurt so deeply. Only after he died did I realize how deeply I could love.

When they told me your brother had died, I needed to pray. Really pray—like I had never prayed before—gut-reaching, down to the darkest corners of my soul prayer. But the only words that would come were "Thank you." I suppose that sounds oddest of all, if I love Christian as deeply as I say. But it was at that moment that so much became clear. It was at that moment that I realized what an awesome and benevolent God we have.

It became a lesson in humanity, this thing called grief. People made it their own. They were willing to share it. This horrendous emotion that defies description, friends and strangers alike would willingly take it upon themselves to help us shoulder it. The seemingly small acts of kindness that strangers and acquaintances performed. The cards, letters, and telephone calls. People we had never met showed up at our door with meals and flowers and kind words. The funeral home donated their services, as did the ambulance service and hospital. Friends and strangers donated to charities in his memory. It all meant so much.

And late one night—one dark wakeful night—a few days after his death, God let me hear for a moment the voices of others as they prayed for us. It was only for a few seconds. All at once I heard several prayers—your grandmother was crying; your aunt prayed in her own unique style; several friends' words of intercession. But then, just as loudly and pronounced were the prayers of people I could not identify. I knew instantly that we had not yet met, but they prayed for us nonetheless. Never believe for a moment your prayers fall on deaf ears. They make more of a difference than we can imagine.

When I called people to tell them Christian had died, the reaction was always the same—that wail. It got so I anticipated it. I would hold the phone away from my ear as soon as I said the words. After a few phone calls, I would forget to whom I was speaking, because behind that inhuman cry, everyone sounded alike. It was a noise like none other I have ever heard and, God willing, never will again.

Your father told me I didn't have to make the calls, but I did. I *needed* to take care of the business and details of his death. For me, it made Christian's death real. And it was not that I did not think your father was strong; it was that I knew how strong I *was*.

His death was unexpected. It was the Monday after Easter that he died. Most of our friends didn't even know Christian was sick. I could not utter the words "Christian died", so instead I said, "We lost Christian." This led to much confusion, as everyone's first reaction was to offer to come "look" for him. In hindsight, I should have chosen my words better, but there were none that seemed adequate.

I told you about how the strangers came and the strangers prayed. But I didn't tell you about the friends.

There are people in our lives that we knew would be there for us, no question about it. Sadly, though, many later confided that they had been *afraid* to see us—afraid they would say the wrong thing or wouldn't know what to say. Some of these people we have known for decades, and they were *afraid* to see us. Fortunately for us, most of them came anyway. Grief does not just affect the parents.

There were also people who surprised us and came, even though it inconvenienced them. Day after day, after work, they would come, driving hours in some cases, to sit up with us, remembering Christian, anticipating our every need, ready to help in whatever way they could. Sometimes, that meant just sitting in silence, other times that meant laughing with us until we cried. But they were there for us.

In most cases, we were too preoccupied to realize what sacrifices people were making. I imagine there are sacrifices some made that I will go to my own grave never fully realizing.

You must remember that people are willing to be there in your time of need. Most people's offers to help are selfless, not selfish. And this is a time to let them help—for them as much as for you. There will be enough lonely days ahead when no one is there.

Ironically, it was on the way to the funeral that I realized that other people in the world were going on with their lives. Silly as it may sound, it was the sight of a mail truck that jarred me back to reality. It actually surprised me to realize that although our lives had been put on hold briefly, the Earth still rotated, and life was still going on, with or without Christian.

Long after the crowds have gone home and the grass has grown over the grave, there is still grief. Mercifully, most days are tolerable and the grief is manageable. But be aware, there are those soul-whipping days, when the grief tears at you and floods your eyes and cramps your gut, even years later. And sadly, those are usually unexpected.

Even now, years after his death, most days I go about life with a business-like competency. Most of the neighbors in our new neighborhood do not even know we have lost a son. It is not that I am denying my boy—though it feels like it sometimes; his name just has not come up yet in conversation, in the year we have lived here. And they do not recognize the grief your father and I carry, such a good job we have done accommodating it into our lives.

Anecdotal note: Christian's funeral was on April 15—Tax Day. Your father, the accountant, had prepared our taxes but had not yet filed our return. After the funeral, he had to ask someone to go to the Post Office to mail it. The irony: in one day we had to deal with Life's Two Inevitables: death and taxes.

FUNERAL AND BEYOND

Infant son, so perfect
Were you an angel
>*Before God plucked you from the Heavens*
>*And laid you in my arms?*

Flawless skin, stretched over baby fat,
Punctuated with dimples in all the right places,
You have your father's best features, and mine.

Nuzzling your neck I smell my milk that
>*Has dripped from your lips and soured*
(On your breath, it still smells sweet.)

Born to a mother who lay crucifix-style,
Named for Our Father's Son,
You've blessed our life beyond words,
>*with only your presence.*

And as you sleep and dream each night,
I say a mother's prayer
>*that He will not decide to return you to your*
>*Heavenly post*
>*and forsake your mortal parents.*

VWV July 23, 1990

18

Let me tell you about your brother's funeral.

I had never planned one before. Except for the wake of a friend's father whom I barely knew, I had not even attended one.

I wanted Christian's funeral to be a celebration of his life. I also knew that most of the hundred or so people attending it had never even met him. So I wanted them to know *who* they were mourning.

The minister read the above poem, written when he was four months old. We laid out a table with his favorite things for viewing. There was the Mickey Mouse raincoat and his black cowboy hat that he never went anywhere without, and his favorite storybooks, and some of his favorite cars, and miscellaneous other toys.

I gave the eulogy. I wasn't sure that I could, but they were my words, and I felt that no one but me should read them. I prayed so hard that God would give me the strength I needed to get through it, and he did. And so with Anneka on my hip, this is what I said:

> *It rained. It rained and it rained and it rained. Quiet, gentle streams of rain. Angels were silently weeping for our loss—even as they rejoiced and welcomed him. And after a night of mournful rain, streaming from the heavens, the sun came up. The puddles dried.*

> *The old man in the backyard went out to tend his garden, like he does every day. The children down the street got up and ate cereal while they watched cartoons. And all the fathers went off to work, briefcases in hand—all but one.*

Somewhere someone's going shopping. Somewhere someone's having a baby. Somewhere an ambulance nears the hospital, siren blaring. And someone else is going through the same thing we are at this very minute.

His Easter basket remains untouched. We threw its contents away this morning. Every corner of his room tells a story. The single sock hanging over the rim of the basketball hoop. The disheveled drawers with clothes half pulled out as I tried to find yet another clean outfit for him to wear after he soiled his last. The bed's unmade. The sheets are dirty—but I won't wash them for a while. Toys are scattered across the floor, beckoning a child to come play. And the walls—beautiful red, green, yellow, and blue cars lovingly stenciled in a make-believe traffic jam; cars which he named "Bobby", each and every one.

Sent to Earth with a divine purpose, Christian accomplished his in only three years and twenty days. The rest of us in this room haven't yet succeeded in that—so maybe he was a little bit closer to perfection than the rest of us. His father says he got his fill of love. He succeeded in touching so many people that he fulfilled his purpose.

As a parent, you try to protect your child. You put plastic covers on the outlets, you lock up the medicines and cleansers. You stock funny Band-Aids and syrup of ipecac, in case of an emergency. You keep them away from the road. You don't let them play with matches or knives.

But you can't protect them from everything. And you realize you can only take precautions.

His sister, whom he adored, misses him, too. And as she grows older, her fourteen months of memories of her big brother will begin to fade. And soon he will become to her a distant memory—that "Boy in those family pictures". But at least she knew him. And in some immeasurable way her life will be affected by his.

And so will all of ours. Maybe not tomorrow, maybe not next week, maybe not in ten years, but someday you'll be reminded of him. Maybe you'll see a tattered black cowboy hat, or a little boy wearing a black and white Mickey Mouse raincoat, or a child with hair the color of Sunshine, whose laugh sounds vaguely familiar, and you'll think of Christian James. And you'll smile. And maybe you'll tell someone else about him and how his short life affected you—and he'll live on.

During the meditation portion of the service, the organ groaned "You Are My Sunshine". That was HIS song. I sang it to him every day of his life. We called him "Sunshine". And at the bottom of his headstone, it reads simply "Our Sunshine". I have never been able to sing that song to any of you girls, even prior to his death. Apparently, though, hearing that song at a child's funeral disturbed some people. Quite a few mentioned later that they would never hear that song again and not think of it the same way. Then it was fitting that it was played.

At his graveside, our minister read "The Runaway Bunny" by Margaret Wise Brown. That too was appropriate because one of his most favorite things in the world was to be read to. And finally, together we all sang "Jesus Loves Me".

The following week we picked out the headstone. I mention that here because it was such a monumental decision (no pun intended). It would be the last thing we could ever give to him. After we left the monument maker's we were so elated (yes, elated), yet sadly, no one in our circle could relate to that. Most of our friends were in their twenties or thirties. Few had buried anyone, let alone a child. So the business of designing a headstone was about as obscure to them as choosing wallpaper border is to a homeless person.

The night before the funeral we held a small, private viewing for a few close friends and family members. There was an entire wall of flowers surrounding Christian's tiny casket. Your father, Larry, and I were first drawn to the flowers, not to where Christian lay. And as we read the cards accompanying the bouquets, Anneka, you climbed up on to the casket, and kissed your brother for the last time. "Bye-bye, She-shin," you said, without any prompting from us. At fourteen months, you had a better grip on death than your parents.

His casket was a pearl gray. The blue and pink calico lining curved around his head, reminding me so much of the infant car-bed that he (and all of you girls) used as babies.

Tucked under his arm is a stuffed "Curious George"—his favorite animal. And pinned to his vest is a small photo of our family then, with the inscription "We love you, Sunshine!" And if memory serves me correctly, there is a small Matchbox car in the casket with him, as well (but I am not positive if that is an actual memory or an afterthought).

He wore his "Daddy suit"—a red vest/black pants ensemble with a polka dot tie (a "big boy tie, like Daddy's", I had told him). I had bought the suit the week before, and he wore it only four days before he died when I had his and Anneka's Easter pictures taken. When I tried the suit on him the night before the pictures, he fought me about taking it off. He threw such a temper tantrum that I had to put one of your Dad's shirts on him, so he could be just like Daddy. Those were the only times he ever wore it, since he was too sick on Easter to go to church. Your father never saw that suit on Christian while he was alive.

An interesting anecdote about that suit: The first time I went to the grocery store after his death, the sandy-haired young man bagging my groceries wore a red vest over a slightly oversized white dress shirt, with a black polka dot tie. Identical to Christian's Daddy's suit in every way except the crest—in its place: a nametag. Although the store uniforms were red, no other employee had a vest—they all wore smocks or jackets. I never saw that young man there again, but I still remember what his nametag read: simply "Chris".

SAYING GOODBYE

How can I tell you what it is like to say goodbye? That would be like describing *blue* to the man who has never seen. But I will try.

I knew the moment your brother died. It was one of the most powerful moments of my life. We were in the ambulance on the way to the hospital. The ride was literally a two-minute car-ride, even without sirens blaring. But I can show you to this day the spot on Ridge Road where his soul left his body.

Nothing physically changed in the ambulance. One paramedic still "worked" on my little boy in the back. Another drove, while he talked to a dispatcher over the radio, in what seemed like some sort of secret code. But something went through me. Your brother, I suppose. And I looked up at the sky at that moment, sure I would see two angels escorting him heavenward. I was actually surprised when I didn't.

But by the time we had gotten to the hospital, a peace had come over me that I can not explain. I'm sure the hospital staff thought I was in some sort of shock. I began referring to Christian in the past tense, even asking if they could "bring him back". They would correct me and say, "No, Mrs. Vanderveen, we're still working on him." But I knew that was futile. (Six months later, I discovered he was actually listed as "D.O.A"—dead on arrival.)

At the hospital, the police and the ER doctor repeatedly questioned me. They would ask me the same questions over and over. Then they would rephrase my answers and try to get me to agree with them. Even at the time, I understood it was to rule out abuse, and I suppose I should have been offended that they would consider ME responsible, but already I knew that it was Christian's time to go. A higher power had already decided that, and no amount of praying or bargaining can change His Will.

Of course, they quickly determined his death to be natural. Somehow when we mentioned that we had brought him to that same hospital for treatment the night before, they quickly became less accusatory and more sympathetic. They even offered to arrange it so we would not have to pay for an autopsy.

At the time, I didn't care if an autopsy was performed or not. It didn't really seem important HOW he died. Or even for that matter, WHY. What was important was that he was gone. It was my mother, your Mammaw, who convinced us to have it done—to rule out something that might put Anneka or any future children at risk. How prophetic, because four years later the doctors would determine that it was a genetic metabolic disorder and that Liesel, who was but a twinkle in her Daddy's eye when Christian died, has it as well. The morning after he died, though, the coroner told us it was Reye Syndrome, even though he had never had aspirin.

We became very involved with the Reye Syndrome Foundation. People gave donations in his memory. A few years later, our family would even be included in a documentary the foundation made for television because his was such a "typical" case.

I can not put into words what it is like to read your own child's autopsy. The first two pages of Christian's are the police report describing pertinent information like my distraught state (*was I distraught enough for them?*) and the cleanliness of our home. (It should be noted here that the only reason that it was clean was because my three-year old tornado had been too sick to play for three days.) The next fourteen pages describe in horrific detail his dissection. Be grateful: I will not describe the rest of the autopsy; suffice it to say, it is gruesome. But how sad that my boy, the child I gave birth to, was reduced to a few pages of medical jargon like some junior high school biology project.

The doctors continued to try to resuscitate him. Each time they would try a new procedure, they would come in to the waiting room, and describe to me in grisly detail the measures they were taking. Finally, I said the words "I don't want him to be a vegetable." And with that the social worker who was with me quietly excused himself and came back with the doctor. "I'm sorry, Mrs. Vanderveen. We did all we could for him," he said. I nodded. They were words I had anticipated hearing ever since that moment in the ambulance.

I will always believe the medical team ceased life-saving efforts because of what I had said. I suppose many people would choose to have their child alive in any condition. And to be honest, I am not sure I would ever make that same choice again, opt for a dead child over an incapacitated one. But Christian was filled with so much life, such vitality; I could not picture him any other way. And for reasons that I will go into later, I had already made peace with his death.

Did I cry? No. Not then. Not right away, at least. And it wasn't shock. Shock implies surprise; there wasn't any. It was…it was…unexplainable. (And here I grasp for a word to describe *blue*.)

They led me and my, now growing, entourage (my mother, my aunt, a friend) to his room. The nurses had put a fresh Johnny-gown on him—

mint green and adorned with a baseball-hat-wearing Mickey Mouse—and removed at least the visible tubes. Gauze patches covered his eyes in the hopes they could be salvaged for donation. (Because it took so long to establish cause of death, we could not donate any of his other organs for transplant.)

The room was dimly lit and my first-born child looked so much like he was sleeping, I waited for his chest to heave. So small, lying in that hospital bed, he looked every bit his three years. I picked him up and sang lullabies to him. I rocked him and kissed him—his mouth, his brow, his fingertips. His golden hair was damp and matted to his head. His skin was cold—so, so cold. When I mentioned that, someone brought me a heated blanket to swaddle him in. I tried to memorize every inch of him, his smell, his feel, his contours. Rigor mortis had set in. But even in death, his fingers closed around my own when I held his hand.

What is it like to know that you will never hug your child again? I can not articulate some things.

COPING

Before losing him,
I believed,
      erroneously,
That I would not go on
      could not go on
      should not go on
          if that ever happened

But then,
I discovered:
      Love is a whole lot bigger than grief
      and there are more sunny days than rainy ones
      and four-leaf clovers are rarer, but sweeter
      and angels really do fly
      and there's glory in fields of dandelions
      and the moon still chases the sun
      and no matter how hard I try,
          nothing will ever happen before its Time
      and however bad it hurts—
         and it will—
            it's far better than the alternative.

VWV May 7, 1996

When you are a parent, please, *PLEASE* don't ever say you won't be able to go on if you ever lose your child (or anything to that effect). Truth is, you may have no choice. People often ask your father and I how we do it, how we go on. The alternatives were limited:

A.)   Have a nervous breakdown.

B.)   Cope.

We chose the latter of the two. Had there been another alternative, we gladly would have entertained it. It was not a momentous decision. But it was a decision, nonetheless. Re-read that sentence: *It was a decision.*

We survived. That is Basic Instinct Number 1: Survival. Even single-celled organisms will attempt to survive at all costs. And so, that is what we did.

I do not, however, look down my nose at those who, for whatever reasons, feel they could not go on in a similar situation. It is not mine to judge, and circumstances are unique. And I must be honest, my own thinking was not always totally rational. I don't like the thoughts I sometimes entertained. But in our case, it was a choice to cope—and a very deliberate one at that.

Conversely, when I meet another bereaved parent, I always look at them in awe and wonder, "How do they go on?" Then soberly, I remember I, too, have survived.

Understand this, my children: there is nothing extraordinary about grieving. However, what someone *does* with his or her grief may be extraordinary.

One of the cruelest (yet well-intentioned) things people say to grieving parents is "At least you have another child." And as painful as those words are, there is an infinite amount of truth in them. We chose to go on for you, Anneka. In some very bleak days—and there were a few—you were our sole purpose for getting up in the morning. You still *needed* us. There were chores to be done and diapers to change and whether I felt like cooking or not, you needed to eat. And later, on those infrequent, but just as difficult days, your sisters also gave us the strength to go on.

It was not all drudgery. Some days I was energized and motivated, surprised by how much I could accomplish. But other days, your father would ask a simple question like, "What did you do today?" and I would have to struggle to think of anything productive I had done. But we got through that.

The day before he died (which, remember was Easter), I had two separate conversations about losing children. Both times, I remember saying (like I had so many other times), "If anything ever happened to one of my children, they better bury me right along with them, because I won't be able to go on." God doesn't like ultimatums—I am sure of that. So somewhere off in the Great Beyond, perched on His Divine Throne, He said, "Wanna bet?"

Well, maybe it didn't work quite like that. But I do honestly believe that He makes all of us confront our worst fears at some point in our lives. Aren't I lucky I've had such soul-enriching fears?

It is amazing what the human spirit can endure. God gives us obstacles, I believe, to challenge the "I cant's" we set up for ourselves.

Sometimes, your father and I would jokingly look heavenward and say out loud, "OK, God, we've done enough growing. We've learned enough. Now you can stop giving us lessons to learn."

WHY?

Once when I was in school, my teacher passed out an essay test. The only question on the test was "Why?" We had an hour to complete it.

I wrote simply, "Because", laid down my pencil, turned my test booklet over, and sat quietly for an hour while my classmates wrote feverishly. I got an "A".

The only other right answer, the teacher later told us, would have been "Why not?"

I don't get bogged down with the "why" of Christian's death. It is not mine to understand. It is far more important for me to know that there *is* a reason Christian died, than to know what it is.

ANNEKA

Little girl dances
to inaudible music.
Gleely spinning,
watching her dress puff out.

Momentarily transfixed,
caught up in her
carefree
two-year-old-ness
  Wish that I were
    As young.

VWV 1995

Anneka, my Anneka,

Too serious for your seven years, you have seen so much tragedy in such a short time. If I could take it all away, just for you, I would. I was an adult before I ever attended a funeral. You were not even out of diapers yet.

You were such a happy baby. It wasn't until I pored over the many photo albums chronicling your childhood, that I realized the transformation you underwent. Your expression: it became so serious after Christian died. Prior to his death, you smiled all the time. Since his death there is a serious, too wise expression behind your eyes. Your entire life now marked by a grief you don't remember.

We—your father, I, everyone—tried to shield you from the grief. We spoiled you after he died—as if material things could assuage your grief. You handled it so maturely, though. Do you know you began speaking in complete sentences the week after he died? At times, you comforted us, instead of the other way around.

When I returned home from the hospital, after he died, the neighbors who had been watching you offered to keep you. But I declined—I *needed* to hold you, to touch you, to feel your heart beat. When they brought you home, I knew I needed to say something to you. You were not yet fourteen months old. *How could I put 'death' into terms you would understand?* I knelt in front of you and said, "Anneka, Christian died. He's gone to live with Jesus and the angels, in Heaven." And you immediately replied, "Bye-bye She-Shin. Bye-bye, Baby." You knew.

Our good friend Miss Lorraine held you when the ambulance pulled away. You were screaming. Nothing would comfort you. But a few minutes later, you dropped your head on her shoulder and your doll to the floor, and fell instantly to sleep. Lorraine asked what time it was—for some reason that seemed urgent to know. It was 3:37 p.m. The same time I "felt" Christian die. The death certificate reads the time of death as 4:10 p.m.—but you and I know better.

The afternoon after he died, you were screaming, inconsolably. No one could figure out what was bothering you so much. Finally, someone set a plate of food in front of you and we realized you were famished. Because we were not hungry, we forgot that you might be. It was a quick lesson in priorities. (And no, we did not make that mistake again.)

I hope you never realized that with every one of your milestones, there was a sadness that Christian never reached the same milestone and that he was not there to witness yours. Nonetheless, that never diminished my pride in you. If only you could see yourself through my eyes, for just one second.

You were not conceived to be the oldest, and yet that is what you are. In respect to birth order, you have been the youngest child, an only child, (technically) a middle child, and now the oldest child. Hopefully, you will reap the benefits of being each.

I asked you once what your earliest memory was. You said playing matchbox cars with Christian—and that you were the airplane. Hold onto that memory. It is one I share with you, for in my mind you are a pudgy toddler giggling and frolicking with your older brother. You looked up to him—and whatever he was doing, you wanted to do, too. It was a special bond between you two. Sometimes, I think you lost your best friend that day.

The only sound more beautiful than the laughter of one of my children, is all of their laughter in unison. You are the only child of mine who has laughed with Christian. You are the bridge between your siblings—and the "before and after" of our family.

You saw him when we couldn't. After he died, you would walk into a room and greet him with, "Hi She-shin!" and a wave.

Once, you almost fell off of the steps onto the driveway. It looked inevitable that you would fall, and I could not get to you in time. But you found your footing, at the last possible second. And then slowly pointed skyward and whispered, "She-shin," as your eyes followed your finger.

There was an irrational, overwhelming urgency to keep his bedroom untouched after he died. Yes, I know that sounds as if I wanted to make it a shrine to him, but that wasn't it at all. Or maybe it was. But you wanted to *play* in there. After his funeral I opened the door for you and you reveled in it. I guess it made you feel closer to him to play with his things. And so I let you. And that was right, too.

Perhaps out of your father's and my emotional state, you developed a need to comfort, to please. On Mother's Day the year you were two, you and I visited the cemetery. By now, you were very much at home there—playing leapfrog over the flush headstones or hide-and-go-seek behind the only oak tree, while I visited Christian's grave.

On this particular day, I was lost in my own grief while you ran around the cemetery. That is, until you returned to me, chubby hands outstretched bearing a gift. "Happy Muffer's Day, Mommy!!" You were beaming—the broadest grin I had seen on you for a very long time. In an earnest attempt to cheer me up, you had searched the grounds for a gift to present to me. Was it a bouquet of dandelions gathered from between the graves? No. A miniature flag off the grave of a vet? No. It was the brass marker from a now anonymous grave. Even then, you could make me smile.

THE MUSIC IN HIS NAME

When parents are expecting a child, they take great care in choosing a name. It is a monumental decision. Some people even believe it determines one's outcome in life. It is the tag which will take us from cradle to grave. But in choosing it, one never expects to *see* it on a headstone.

Christian James Vanderveen
March 23, 1990—April 12, 1993

It is a deafening experience to lose a child. As if not hearing his laugh anymore isn't enough, not to call his name anymore is a tragedy. The sound of it is music. Acquaintances rarely will say it, even if they know it. Friends often sidestep using it too, for fear the mere mention of his name will evoke tears, or the Wrath of God, or smite them the same misfortune. But for the parent who has lost a child, to hear his name is music. It is a grand symphony, and the song of angels. Yet the sound of it makes others uncomfortable. So we avoid even uttering his name at times. More was taken from us than just a child.

Christian.

Your brother's name was chosen the day after he was born. Certain he would be a girl, we had not yet settled on a boy's name. It was neither your father's nor my favorite name, at the time. But it was the only one to appear on both of our lists as acceptable. It upset some Jewish relatives that we chose to name him *Christian*, but that was not our intention. His middle name is after your grandfather, my father. (Grandpa's name was actually "Jimmy Lee".)

Christian James.

We broke tradition on your father's side. In the Dutch culture, the eldest son is named for the father's father, the second son for the mother's father, the eldest daughter for the mother's mother, and so on. It really did not come up as an issue when naming him. But months after he died, your father confided that he felt if we had followed tradition, he would have lived. Grief is so often irrational.

Christian James Vanderveen.
The first, the last, the only.

HUMOR

God has a sense of humor. And lucky for you, your parents are the punch-line to the Great Cosmic Joke. On those days when everything seems to go wrong, or the absurd abounds, sometimes I am sure I can hear God snickering somewhere off in the distance.

But it is with a sense of humor that we got through the darkest times of our lives. Grief doesn't stop when the body is in the ground. Nor a year later, nor ten years later. It is a definition of life, not a disease that one recovers from. And usually, it strikes without warning, when you least expect it. So your father and I dealt in the only way we knew how: by making jokes. At times, I suppose our humor was blasphemous and perhaps distasteful. But I believe God wanted us to get through Christian's death with our sanity in tact. So that is how we did it.

Nowhere had I ever heard that it was appropriate to laugh when grieving, but it felt natural. No one ever said, it's OK to laugh and cry at the same time. So, I'm giving you permission here to feel a thousand emotions at once. I laughed and I cried on my wedding day. I laughed and I cried when I became a mother. I laughed and I cried the night Christian died.

The night he died, Larry and I stayed up late, talking and laughing. It wasn't the first time in our marriage we had done that, but there was something different that night. It was cleansing to laugh. We needed to laugh to remember. It felt right. Being able to laugh was reassuring: dark as the night was, there would be a dawn.

The next day as friends and family gathered in our kitchen, someone complimented your father, the gardener, on how green the houseplants were. "Yea, we can keep the plants alive, just not our kid," one of us quipped. Your father and I roared hysterically. There was a long, shocked pause from those closest to us before they saw the humor and joined us.

Another time, a few months after his death, I had to leave church during a hymn, because I could not stifle a case of the giggles. The reason: the lyrics were, "Jesus said, Christian follow me". And I found the irony ludicrous.

CROCODILE TEARS

So special was Christian James, he did not just belong to your father and I. And neither did the grief when we lost him.

But there were a few people who, I suspect, made more show of their grief than necessary. And there were a few. I tell you this now not to degrade anyone, but to warn you. In the future, you may attend a funeral and you may witness the carrying-on of some people. I am not talking about the honest-to-God, passionate grief that is uncontrollable. That is unmistakable. But there were people—people close to us—that made a mockery of our pain. In some respect, some of them, made a competition out of proving who hurt the most. Let me tell you something, it was your father and I who hurt the most—and who loved him the most.

There was the well-intentioned sympathizer who claimed she knew how I felt because SHE had been Christian's mother in a *previous* life. And, of course, the suggestion, only hours after he had died, that we get pregnant as soon as possible. (In case there is any doubt, grief is not the aphrodisiac the soap operas lead you to believe.) There was also the woman who got drunk at our house and sadly admitted to us that she believed it was HER son who was supposed to have died, not ours. It was even suggested—by someone who I am sure believed whole-heartedly—that he died because I had not prayed enough for his healing.

And several others who cried "Crocodile tears" and made their grief a show, not for Christian, but I believe, so others close to us would say, "Gee

THEY are taking Christian's death especially hard." To be honest, that false grief disgusted me.

Let there be no question about it, your father and I grieved just as hard and deeply as everyone else did. Privately. We just did not make a show of it. A few days after his death, my own mother even asked if we had cried yet. Of course we had. But there is a time and a place for all things—even grief.

Even recently—now six years later—it has been suggested to me that your father and I were thought to be "heartless" by some for not making a show of our emotions at your brother's funeral. Unless someone has walked a mile in my shoes, they can not judge me. I do not need to justify ANY feeling to another living soul. My God and I know what I have gone through in this lifetime—and I will be judged accordingly when the time comes.

Some people show their grief loudly, for all the world to witness. Others, privately. And still others grieve the way they believe it is expected of them. I do not want you to be cynical or suspicious, just know that sometimes things are not the way they may appear.

I have to be brutally honest, at times I felt I was consoling others and I resented it. I did what I could, but at times I had to walk away, because I just didn't have anything left to give anyone else. Because Larry and I were "doing so well" handling our emotions, people leaned on us. Odd, isn't it? I suppose we should take that as a compliment. But somehow being the "strong one" all the time gets exhausting.

My first priorities were Anneka and Larry, your father. Period. Anneka NEEDED me. She was still a baby—fourteen months old. She had lost her big brother and I couldn't explain to her in terms she could understand what was gong on. But maybe she understood best of all...

And your father, I had never witnessed such pain, which is why the aforementioned false show of grief was so insulting.

I wish I could tell you that I am a big enough person—or a faithful enough Christian—not to have been bothered by the pettiness of it all. I can not. Your parents are human. We have our faults. And like others, we feel indignation at what we perceive to be injustice. That others would "envy" our grief is appalling. And I have to be truthful about that.

Maybe, in retrospect, they thought they were being supportive. I don't know. Just be aware that those who may cry the loudest or make the biggest show when someone dies—perhaps it is genuine, perhaps they have ulterior motives.

YOUR FATHER

Husband,

> *Will you still hold my hand*
> *when we're*
> *a hundred and two and three,*
> *while we amble on walks*
> *with Teflon joints*
> *and aluminum canes?*
> *Will you be by my side*
> *when our children*
> *are grandparents,*
> *several times over?*
>
> *And when my mind wanders,*
> *back to our youth,*
> *will you still be there to travel with?*
> *And when there is no one*
> *left who*
> *remembers all we've been through,*
> *will you still wink at me,*
> *with your **good** eye?*
>
> *And someday, when I prattle on,*
> *due to old age,*
> *not just youthful enthusiasm,*

will you still pretend to listen,
even if you don't always hear?

And lastly,
when I lay on my deathbed,
and list my regrets,
and joys,
(and pray that I was the woman
I always wanted to be)
and thank the Lord
for the man I was a child with
and a bride to
will you hold my hand
until life departs,
or instead,
will you wait for me
on the Other Side,
after you've gone ahead
to prepare Heaven for me?

VWV Jan. 28, 1994

He is a strong man, your father. His strength was one of the first things that attracted me to him. It was one of the ways he measured up to your grandfather. After twelve years of marriage, my heart still jumps when I hear his car pull up. He is the first one I call with good news—and with bad. He fills in the details of memories that have begun to fade. And he understands, without further explanation, when I say simply, "I am sad today."

But when he said goodbye to his only son, his body rocked with sobs and he wailed, "*WHY?!!! People don't die from the flu!!*" I had no answers. I have never felt as powerless.

There were times when we clung to each other in grief. But, too, during the first few months following his death, especially, there were times we grieved independently. Neither one of us could be strong for the other. On days when I ached for no other reason than having lost a child, I could not understand why the things that bothered me most seemed to have no effect on him. And vice versa.

They say there is an extremely high percentage of grieving parents who divorce. I understand. You lash out at the ones you love the most. Even marital relations were not the same as they were before.

It is not my intention to share with you the intimate details of your father's and my sex life. What goes on behind closed bedroom doors, should stay there. But in all the grief books I have read, never did any address that. Someday, God forbid, you and your spouse may go through the same pain. And I want you to understand that even those sexual feelings you may be having are not a betrayal of your loved one.

I did not think your father and I would ever be able to resume our intimacy, but we did. And our lovemaking had a new purpose. The passion that we once shared was now a release. For months, I cried after we made love. That is difficult to admit. And it was not a real ego-builder for your father, either. But that is where I was emotionally.

Eventually, our marriage took on a normalcy. Although, it was not—nor will it ever be—the same. It evolved. We now share something in common that no one else can know—the pain and the recovery of losing our only son. Close as our friends and family may be, it was not *their* son who died on April 12, 1993.

There is a comfort in knowing you have gone to the brink of Hell with someone and made it back. Make no mistake, it was Hell. And there is no one I would rather travel there with, than your father.

It is important that you know how your father found out about Christian's death. His reaction shows the depth of character this man possesses.

The morning of April 12, 1993, Larry left for New York City where he was to work that week—150 miles from our home in Connecticut. It was not uncommon in those days for your father to travel with his government job. In fact, we usually only saw him on weekends.

He deliberated about going to work that day, but Christian seemed to be improving, so he couldn't really justify staying home. I kept him posted throughout the day on your brother's progress.

A little after three, your father was outside the credit union where he was working, having a cigarette. The song *"Cat's in the Cradle"* was playing from a radio somewhere. The song moved him since the lyrics describe how a father was not around much when his son was growing up and eventually they ran out of time together. Just then, someone came and told your father he had to get home right away.

Unbeknownst to me, he had borrowed a car phone. Minutes after Christian was pronounced dead, the hospital switchboard operator came running in to our private waiting room. "The dad's on the phone; he's calling from a car phone from a traffic jam in New York." (Knowing he didn't have a cell phone in his car, I had visions of him going from car to car, knocking on windows, asking to borrow a phone from fellow drivers.)

The room was filled with people—doctors, social workers, police, nurses, the hospital chaplain, my aunt. We argued for a few minutes over what to do. "Tell him to pull over and we'll have the State Police bring him the rest of the way," suggested the policeman. "We can't tell him. Tell him we're still working on the boy," said the doctor. Everyone had an opinion. He still had a two-and-a-half hour drive. It was my decision. I could not lie to your father. That would be unfair. But I could not be the one to tell him either.

The chaplain very graciously offered to break the news to him. He said a silent prayer, while he composed himself—I imagine searching for the right words. "This is the hospital chaplain, Mr. Vanderveen. I'm sorry. We did all we could for him."

And then I took the phone. And your father's first words to me, upon hearing that his firstborn had died were, "Oh Vicki, *are you alright?*" I was surrounded by an entire support system. Your father was by himself, in a traffic jam near LaGuardia Airport, on a borrowed car phone, and his first concern was for *me*.

It was a profound moment. That solidified what I already knew—what a truly special man he is. To this day, when I am angriest with him or feeling particularly unloved, I remember those words. They are the sweetest—no, *bitter*sweetest—words I will ever hear.

MARRIAGE

We embraced—
        not like we had a thousand times before
        but this time in grief

Angel tears fell from heaven
        mingled with our own

We became one—
        one man
        one woman
            coupled in
                one child lost.

While the world spun,
        time obliged and stood still with us,
                united in the grief of our only son.

VWV

One of the greatest fallacies of our time is that marriage is 50/50. It is not. It never has been. It never will be. Some days it will be 60/40, some 90/10, and on some really horrendous days: 105/-5. Depending on who has the greatest need at that moment, you may find yourself giving and giving and giving, because that is what is needed of you. But be assured, there will be a day when you can do nothing but take. And if you're really lucky, most days you'll meet somewhere close to the middle. It is the wise adult who can understand this.

When your grandfather, my father, died, it was a different state in our marriage than when Christian died. Your father was sympathetic, and though he had lost a father-in-law, it was not his parent for whom he grieved. And he could be there for me—unconditionally—without expecting me to support him or to give to him. He could be—and was—unselfish and supportive. And I could *receive*. I suppose that is the biggest difference between losing *our* child and losing *my* parent.

The crises in our marriage since Christian's death—and in like all marriages, there have been a few, some unrelated to his death, some related to it—somehow seem so trivial in perspective, no matter how catastrophic they might have seemed prior. In God's Infinite Wisdom, He doesn't halt all the other issues, just because you're grieving: the phone bill still appears in the mailbox every month and holidays still need to be negotiated and work still demands attention. Somehow, you go on.

Marriage is like a dance. The movements, the rhythm so well choreographed and rehearsed that the music is silent. The partners know each other so well, they move accordingly in anticipation to the other's needs. I have witnessed even divorced couples move in a silent dance.

Your father and I are no different. We "pick up the slack" for the other, when we can. When one of us is feeling especially vulnerable, we tread lightly. But hardest are those days when we are both down; when neither one of us can pick up the slack. It is not always possible to stroke someone's ego, or bolster their mood, when you yourself need that. Gratefully, those Hellish days are infrequent. We have traveled so far since the early days after your brother's death.

Marriage is also like a container. There are times when your father is the fluid that fills the gaps that I leave—where I end he begins—and together we fill the container. And like a container, the contents are constantly changing.

My mother gave me the best piece of advice regarding marriage years ago—long before I was a bride. Know that some days you will wake up more in love with your partner than other days. Immense truth, when you keep in mind that love is at the core. Some days, love is the rush of newlyweds, and some days, it is the quiet in being accustomed to another. And sometimes, those days are only hours apart.

EMOTIONS

Benefited by being a Navy brat, as a child, I had the fortune of living in different parts of the country. In my travels, I discovered that everyone has the same palette of emotions regardless of gender, nationality, class, color—or strange, unintelligible accent.

Imagine, each of us is issued a paint-box with all the same colors in it—red, blue, yellow, green, orange, purple. Because each of us mixes our colors differently, the shades vary. One person hasn't used his blue yet, so it is more brilliant than the next. Another has mixed his red with the yellow and so it has an orange tint to it. Some have watered theirs down.

Emotions are like the colors in the paint-box. Here is the lesson: it is how we deal with those emotions that make us different. Never, for a second, believe that you are alone in how you feel, or that you love deeper, or have more rage, or feel more passion. It is your responsibility, and only yours, to determine what you do with that rage or love or pain or joy or grief or passion. You are accountable for every action you take.

I could absolutely justify any action with "Because I lost a child." I choose not to. Just because I *can* would not make it *right*. I am responsible for every decision I make in my life, and every decision I make effects someone else. Just as yours do.

Many crimes have been committed and wrongs justified because people forget that others share the same emotions they do.

If I can teach you only one lesson in my lifetime, this is the lesson I choose for you.

KATRINA

February 10, 1998

Dear Katrina,

> *You're grieving now for*
> *the brother you never knew*
> *and*
> *you want to know all there*
> *was about him,*
> *so maybe,*
> > *in your three-year-old mind*
> *you can find some connection*
> *to another three-year-old,*
> > *besides the parents who*
> > *brought you both into the world.*

> *I ache for you—*
> > *and for your fresh grief.*
> *Though it has been five years,*
> > *almost, now,*
> > *since we left him at Pine Grove,*
> *it's all new to you—*
> > *newly cognizant of what death*
> > ***really** means,*
> > > *not just the platitudes*

53

we've fed you since you were born.
We thought you understood—
foolish us.
Forgive us.
He was merely two-dimensional
in your mind's eye.

Let me see if I can make
him more alive for you:
he was all that a child is.
He was joy personified,
he was peanut butter on a spoon
and matchbox cars,
and cowboy hats.

He was, more times than not,
in his own world,
and he was belly laughs
and pouts so animated
*they made **you** smile.*

He was hugs,
and unidentifiable stickiness
and sweetness after a bath.

He was mud puddles
and music
and raincoats
(even on sunny days)
and playing grown-up.

He was more belly laughs.

He was soft breath
　　　and the smell of outdoors.
He was wisdom incarnate
　　　and he was all things new.
He was curiosity
　　　and he was storybooks.

He was Lego towers
　　　whose only purpose were to be destroyed.
He was sitting time-out
　　　and quiet late-night snuggles.
He was "everything is an adventure"
　　　and he was dance in all movement.
He was Peter Pan,
　　　the boy who never grew up.

He was, Oh God,
　　　what is the word I'm searching for?
　　　　He was Christian,
　　　　　your brother.
　　　And he is alive in you.
　　　　And we love him.
　　　　　And we love you, too.

Mommy

VWV 1998

My Katrina,

At three, you seemed, all at once, to realize that your brother had died before you had a chance to know him. It was heart-wrenching. You searched the house for pictures—*any* picture that had you and he together. And sadly, there were none. You begged us to re-paint your room the way he had had it. And you sobbed, as if he had just died.

Perhaps, it was because I was pregnant (with Annelies) and you made the connection that the baby in my tummy that you could not see was your sibling just like Anneka and Liesel and, even Christian. Maybe you had a dream about him. Maybe you fed off of some pain your father or I were projecting. I don't know. But it was out of the blue and we were not prepared for this new-found grief. Even our minister and your pre-school teachers could not give us any guidance.

You are the child of mine who draws rainbows, and, like a rainbow, you were the brightness after the storm—full of color, full of Hope. We became pregnant with you almost immediately after he died. The promise of a new child gave us—all of us—something to look forward to.

Never once, Katrina, did I want you to replace Christian. Nor have I EVER wished you were him. It is infinitely important to me that you believe that.

From the beginning, you were a happy baby—cooing and smiling almost immediately after birth. And your gift of laughter has brightened more than one cloudy day. It was as if God knew what child we needed at that time in our lives, and He chose you for us.

> *In the still of*
> *the early morning twilight hours*
> *I hold my*
> *not-yet day old child*

and now
put a face, and a name, and a gender
to the kicks and rumbles
of my belly.

Hours old
yet already
a complete person
with an identity
and a purpose
and a character.

I marvel at
her innocence
and wisdom
and potential

And somehow,
I know God
is smiling down
through the
heavens at us.

VWV March 14, 1994

REMEMBERING

I could fill volumes with the most minute details of Christian's death, but I won't. Because you see I can remember every moment of his last days, and yet I can't. Sometimes a memory comes rushing at me with such force, that I can relive it with every cell of my being and every sense I possess and *I am there again*. And other times, I can't recall a single detail that is on the tip of my recollection—it makes me want to scream!

They say time heals all wounds. I suppose it does anesthetize the senses, to some degree. But there is a cruel side-effect. Memories that once were so vivid—so tangible—now dim. One of the saddest parts about losing a child is how hard it is to recall those memories.

I can't recall things like Christian's favorite flavor birthday cake (I *believe* it was chocolate), or his last words to me (he yelled out the word "Pain" a few minutes before he died—I did not even think he knew what that word meant; and I cringe when I think of that because I don't recall if he said anything after that), or if he ever tasted rock candy, or climbed a tree...or...or...*What else has my memory deprived of me?*

But I do remember his favorite foods were oranges and fruit roll-ups and his least favorite was kale. His favorite color was red and his favorite car was a Corvette—specifically, Pake's red Corvette. He went trick-or-treating exactly twice in his brief lifetime—once as an M&M, once as Pinocchio. And I can still see the look on his face when he received his Cozy Coupe, from Mammaw.

I remember the feel of his hugs, and the warm breath that would escape his lips just as he drifted off to sleep, and the sparkle in his eye when he thought he was getting away with something, and, most precious of all, what he sounded like when he said "I love you".

Since Christian's death, I do not wish away my children's childhoods anymore. I spent too many of Christian's too-few days looking forward, instead of enjoying the present. I realize too well, today may be the only day I have with you. I cringe when I hear other parents say, "I can't wait until she's out of diapers!" or "I can't wait until he's able to…" There is a splendor in every age, and I try to enjoy each one—from Annelies' new discoveries to Liesel's curious imagination to Katrina's sophisticated humor to Anneka's budding maturity.

In addition, I don't take for granted my memories anymore. I try to imprint little things about each of you into my memory. I have memorized where every freckle is on your bodies, and the shape of your fingernails, and the smell of your hair after a bath, and the smell of your sweat after really hard play, and how you carry your shoulders, and the specks of color in your irises, and the melody of your laughter, and what makes each of you unique. They are each different, you know. Five children I have, and five pairs of different colored eyes they have—five laughs, five hugs, five scents, five individuals.

And five different perspectives of the same mother. Someday, if I am lucky, you girls will sit around remembering me. You'll relate the same stories about me, but you'll each remember them differently. That's good. Share. It will help you to remember.

GRATITUDE

I could:
Sit in the dark—
> *be miserable,*
> *surround myself with gray*
> *and wallow.*

Instead,
I choose
To open the drapes—
> *even if the neighbors are out*
And turn on all the lights—
> *despite the electric bill.*
And surround myself
> *with as many colors*
> *as I can—*
>> *even if they don't match.*

Because
That's the way I like it
And
Who can be miserable
> *in a rainbow?*

VWV

When he died, I often questioned what I would have done differently had I known Christian was going to die. I have concluded that I am grateful—if I can use that term—that he died in exactly the way he did.

I have talked with parents who *had* the opportunity to know their children would die (sometimes waiting for years), and it seems to me I am not strong enough to live that roller-coaster. I suppose I would have dealt the best way I knew how, if that is what God had chosen for Christian. And I suppose there is a blessing in being able to say goodbye. But gratefully, he was taken suddenly.

And because his death was a natural one, I didn't have to contend with the blame and guilt that would be inevitable had he died an accidental death.

I suppose I could fault others for his death—the ambulance driver, the doctors, myself, God. I choose not to. I am grateful I have made my peace with that.

I am grateful for the time I had with him.

I am grateful for each one of you girls. In your eyes, I see the promise of the future.

I am grateful for your father.

I am grateful for every hug I had from Christian.

I am grateful I can account for every moment of Christian's life, and in every moment, there was not one that he was not with someone who loved him.

I am grateful I *knew* him.

I am grateful that of all the mothers in the world, God chose to give him to me.

I am grateful for choosing to go on with my life after losing Christian—otherwise I would never have had or known you, Katrina, Liesel, and Annelies. And I am grateful I had Anneka to "ground" me when Christian died.

I am grateful for my faith that I didn't really know I had until it was tested.

I am grateful for fistfuls of dandelions and four-leaf clovers and maple-syrup kisses and sleeping babies and colored-chalk drawings and sunrises and Cesarean sections and matchbox cars and watermelon slices and spontaneous picnics and children's laughter and sweet dreams and locks of hair and the wind that carries memories.

I am grateful for all the lives one little boy touched in such a short period of time.

I am grateful for friends who listened to me babble, when that is what I needed most, and listened to me remember when it was too difficult to do it alone.

I am grateful I am able to find things to be grateful for, after losing a child.

I am grateful for a kind and benevolent God, who could empathize with me, because He, too, lost a son.

I am most grateful for Peace.

REGRETS

I have only one regret: We have a bookcase full of photo albums, but because I was always the one behind the camera there are few photographs of me alone with Christian, and none of us together in his last months.

Inalienable Truths

The sun will rise tomorrow.

If you are lucky enough to have one really close companion to share your pain with, you are golden. If you have a half dozen, you are platinum.

Don't blame.

Don't feel guilty.

Don't be angry.

You can't sue God.

Prayer works.

No matter how much medical intervention or prayer there is, if it's not in God's Plan, it doesn't matter.

It *IS* better to have loved and lost than never to have loved at all.

People really do care.

Strangers are sometimes the best friends you can have.

It is not enough to *have* faith; you must *live* your faith.

I believe everyone senses when the end of their life is near—regardless of how they die.

No one dies alone—even if there is no one there to witness his or her death.

Death is not the ending of a person's existence.

Love does not die, even if the body does.

Grief is, by definition, a selfish emotion.

It is OK to allow yourself to wallow in self-pity—*occasionally.*

Grief is a process. It does not act the same way ten years after you've lost someone as it does the day after.

No matter how brief a person's lifetime is, like the ripples from a pebble cast in a pond, it makes an indelible imprint on the world.

Grief will intrude into your life unannounced and unexpectedly—even decades later.

No matter how close two people are, their grief will never run parallel. Keep that in mind.

Don't get stuck on "why"—it doesn't matter anyway, and you will never be intellectually developed enough to understand anyway.

Emotions are sometimes irrational. Accept that.

No matter how bad things get, remember somewhere, someone else is going through something far worse than you are.

Grief is not an entitlement; you are entitled to grieve, but it does not entitle you to anything else.

No matter what you have lost, you still have much to be grateful for.

As much as I would like to protect you from this emotion called grief, someday you will have to make your own peace with it. It is the difference between watching a football game, and playing in it.

Grief will be different with every person you lose.

There are no short cuts in grief.

When someday you stand by my grave, as much as you may hurt—and you will—know that this is the natural sequence, for a child to bury his parent. And I would gladly give up my life a thousand times over rather than bury another child.

I am the luckiest person in the world.

The sun will set tonight.

HOLIDAYS

The sunshine that you brought us
Has neither dimmed nor waned
And though life has gone on,
It will never be the same.

For three years, we were fortunate
To have you by our side,
But then, the Lord called you
Back to heaven to reside.

Oh, Happy Day, my son,
Today you're turning four
Best wishes, all our love
Forever, ever more.

VWV March 23, 1994

You will, I pray, never know the work I put into holidays after Christian's death. You girls are still small—you need the magic of childhood with Santa Claus, and Easter Bunnies, and Tooth Fairies, and birthday parties. And I need to do it. Perhaps I have overcompensated in my zeal to make meaningful memories for you. And I apologize now if ever in my quest for the perfect holiday, my stress diminishes your excitement. It is, and has always been, with love that I plan the holidays. Know that my intentions are good even if the outcome sometimes lack the anticipation.

It is the time of year, consistently, when I anticipate mourning: the holidays. Easter, especially, is the hardest day of the year. And every year, to this day, I paste on a smile, ogle over the loot the Easter Bunny has left for you, and muddle through church services and a family dinner.

For Christians around the world, Easter is the holiest day of the year. Our Savior rose from the dead that day, and we celebrate, even two thousand years later. For me, it is the bleakest. There is a part of me, in all honesty, that says to God every Easter, "If you could resurrect your son, why not mine?" And I mean it.

Though it falls on different Sundays every year, Easter reminds me of your brother. You see, when I was pregnant with Christian, he was due on Easter. He was Baptized during Lent. His last healthy day was Good Friday. And his last full day of life was Easter. He died on Bright Monday.

Halloween is another difficult day. I had never given that day much thought, before his death: make a costume, hand out candy, over-indulge in Snickers bars, end of holiday. But since his death, I worry that some prankster will deface his grave. I abhor the gruesome costumes—the witches, the ghosts, things like that. *How do I make peace with a harmless children's holiday when all I see irreverence to the dead?*

And March 23. Christian's birthday. It always precedes Easter. I ache for him especially on that day. I give myself permission to mourn on that day. You see, that is also the day I became a mother. And so, it is like applauding with only one hand. *How tall would he be now? What gifts would he request? Would the boy across the street be his best friend now? What would a nine-year old Christian sound like?*

Then there is April 12, each year. His anniversary. Only another grieving parent can understand what that anniversary is like. Marking the passing of another year since his last hug, his last laugh, his last touch.

As your mother, I don't want you to ever know how hard holidays since his death have often been. But when you are adults, I want you to understand, so that, maybe, if ever you are in a dark period of your life, you will find something—anything—to inspire you to make an effort.

CHRISTIANNEKATRINANNELIESEL

Your father wears a gold band on his right hand, inscribed with these letters: "CHRISTIANNEKATRINANNELIESEL" (the names *Christi*an, *Anne*ka, *Katrin*a, *Anne*lies, and *Liesel* minus duplicate letters). It is only slightly a coincidence that all of your names overlap. We did not discover the coincidence until after Katrina was named. When Liesel was named, I was afraid the chain was broken; but we named the youngest of you Annelies (a name your father had pushed for for several daughters) and that connected the other names. I always want you to remember that you are connected to one another, in more ways than one.

Children of mine, you could have been twins—or quintuplets, for that matter—had you not been conceived at different moments. A matter of Fate.

And though the younger of you have older, more experienced parents, we are one family—one that has evolved through the years. Remember this: Christian has touched your lives in immeasurable ways, even though you may not have a conscious memory of him or may not have been born yet when he lived. The mother that you know now is not the same mother that Christian knew. I am wiser, a little bit sadder, and a lot less naïve.

I am the mother of five. People often see my daughters and ask if we are going to try for a boy. That is probably the hardest question to hear; second, maybe only to "How many children do you have?"

I have a son. I have dealt with the circumcision dilemma. I have tried potty-training a boy. I have watched my husband as a child in the play of our son. And I have attempted to raise a gentleman.

But strangers don't see that. They see my four daughters—the girls that I often dress in matching outfits, to celebrate their sisterhood.

I am proud of all of you. I have never wished any of you were not you. Yes, Christian is special to me because he is my son and he has died. But each of my daughters is special in her own right. I watch you and I see a different part of me in each of you—the best parts of me, in you. Sometimes, it is like I am looking through your eyes. I relish your accomplishments and your individuality. But I do not love any of you more than the other—not even Christian. I love him differently. When you are parents, you will be able to understand how you can love several children differently, and the same.

To me, you are all equal pieces of a pie. In fact, in my mind's eye, I picture us all in a circle holding hands—yes, even Christian. That way I can see him with all of you. A complete family—the way it was meant to be (at least the way I think it should be). It is a beautiful sight.

LIESEL

This child,
        so familiar, and yet, a stranger.
Our first meeting is
        not like making a new friend,
        but more
            like being reacquainted with a best friend
                after a long absence—
                    just like the others before her.

Nuzzling her,
        the scent is so familiar
        it awakens a long lost memory,
            just out of reach.
I know her velvety-smooth skin,
        before we touch.
My palms mimic
        the subtle nuances and contours
            that are her body's.

There is something primal about
        this meeting,
            and something original.

And after she is whisked away,
        I recognize her cry,

having heard it only once.

She is mine…
And I am hers.

And we will share a lifetime
re-learning all there is to know
about the other.
And I will relish it.

VWV May 1996

Little Lady Liesel,

Even as I write this, you have only recently past the milestone of your brother's oldest age. Of all my children, it is probably the greatest milestone for you. You are the child who most resembles Christian James. There have been times I have been caught off-guard by the resemblance. Sometimes, I shudder when I watch you sleep. And you are the child of mine who has been diagnosed with the same disease that in all likelihood took your brother's life.

When you were diagnosed with a genetic metabolic disorder, I felt like I had lost Christian all over again, and worse, the possibility that I could lose you as well. By then, I had made peace with Christian's death four years before. And in some conceited way, I had always assumed that since God had taken one of my children, the rest of my children would be spared. Now the reality of my naivete set in.

It has been suggested to me, on several occasions, that perhaps your brother died so that you could live. I disagree. I tell you this not to guilt you about your own life, but to prepare you. Your brother lived—as you do, as I do—with a purpose. Every moment of his life, beginning with his conception, was a miracle. As is yours.

True, because of Christian's death, we are aware of the metabolic disorder you have. But I have never believed that your life—or anyone else's, for that matter—was contingent on someone else's life. Irony of ironies, your brother was the healthiest person I had ever known, prior to his death. That probably was what kept him alive for three years and twenty days.

I look at his life as a gift. As much as I am loathe to admit it, there was a time—before I was a grieving parent—that I looked at a child's death as a waste of life. When we were in college, the twenty-one-year-old resident assistant of your father's died in a car crash, a few days after the semester ended. At the time, I remember thinking his life had been wasted, and that his parents had wasted all that money on tuition. I am ashamed of myself. No life is a waste.

Most days, I do not think about the possibility of losing you—or rather, I do not dwell on it. But it is always in the back of my mind. I feel more prepared now, then when you were first diagnosed. And with few exceptions, your father and I try to raise you like your sisters—like we did with your brother: with the assumption that we are raising you to become a gracious, productive adult.

But when you get ill, it is another story. You wilt. And I am reminded too well how quickly my life could change again, and just how precious yours is. I do not sleep when you are ill. I hover. I wring my hands. I check on you constantly. I am in constant prayer—pleading, begging, bargaining. I can not do enough for you then. Most days, I tell myself I am strong. But when you are sick, I realize how weak I am. I can not heal you. I could not heal your brother. You are vulnerable, and I pray for God's mercy.

Your grandmother says out of all of my children, you are the one most like me. You have your own way of doing things. You march to your own drummer.

One night a few months ago, we were eating dinner when you jumped up and shouted, "Christian's outside! I saw him!" Your father and I looked at each other, and mouthed to one another, "She saw her own reflection." But you insisted—and even described his hat and Mickey Mouse raincoat to a tee. I know enough not to doubt my children when they say they have seen their brother.

Someday, I pray, I will hold *your* child in my arms. And you will be a new mother, trying to make sense of it all. So I will share with you now the Great Secret of Parenting: the child is the teacher, not the parent; and you will learn more in one day from your children, than you could teach them in a lifetime.

PERSPECTIVE

As I have said before, grief is a process. And I am not at the same place in it that I was a year ago, or two years ago, or six years ago. It is an ongoing evolution—much like education. As an infant, you begin learning before you take your first breath. That education does not stop when someone places a rolled-up sheepskin in your palm.

The following was my perspective one month after Christian's death. I include it so that you can see for yourself what one-month into the evolution reveals. I can not say that every word that follows is how I feel today, but it is how I felt less than five weeks after he died.

"Headstone" should not be in any child's vocabulary. Yet our fifteen-month old knows that word, as well as "cemetery", and a few other rather morbid words that even I never thought I'd use comfortably in a sentence.

Where our family outings used to include trips to the zoo or picnics, now we visit her brother's grave. His plot is tucked neatly under a big oak tree—the kind an old wood and rope swing should hang from—but close enough to the road to watch the cars he loved so much. Another little boy is buried next to him.

The other children in the cemetery, I imagine, are Christian's heavenly playmates. The older souls buried nearby: his adopted guardians.

There's even the grave of a seven-year-old not far from the driveway where we park. It's my favorite (if I can use that term). You see, someone who loves that little boy very much planted two pinwheels on his grave. Whenever I pull up, one of the pinwheels always twirls— even when the wind is still. Sometimes both are whirring. I like to think it's the boys' way of waving at me. I always wave back and smile.

Grief is not necessarily a dirty word—or a bad thing. Even prior to his death, I knew I was blessed. But still I took so much in my life for granted. Not until one is shocked out of complacency, do we realize what we have. Death does that.

*My own experience with death is limited. I had never planned a funeral before. And for the months before our first child was born, when we poured over countless baby-name books, and so lovingly chose his name—Christian James Vanderveen—**never** did we consider how it would look on a headstone.*

Christian's sister plays among the graves, weaving in and out of headstones, stopping only to smell a flower or to finger a tiny flag. I walk around reading the names; righting an overturned potted plant here and there; commenting out loud, or silently, how much this one or that must have been loved and still is; remembering people I've never met.

Even now, many of the graves are newly decorated with Mother's Day gifts—wreathes with "Mother" banners or a bouquet of favorite flowers.

For me, cemeteries are not sad places. Rather, they are places to ponder the "Now", not dwell on the "Was" or "If only...".

My mother, too wise for her forty-something years, has always said, "No one is promised tomorrow." Usually, I heard this when sulking or nursing a grudge—her way to get my sister and me to stop a feud (though it usually didn't work). Still, lately I've been reminding myself of her words.

Someday I will be reunited with my child. Never was a child loved more. Well, maybe **one** was (a couple thousand years ago) or at least **by** more. But I digress.

Parents who have lost children ten or forty or fifty years ago, still refer to that child as a child. And Christian will always be my three-year-old. Even as his sister, God willing, turns two, then three, then forty, he will still be three to us.

I don't know how the hierarchy in Heaven works. The neighbor children asked their parents if Christian will grow up in Heaven, or stay three. None of us knew the answer. I guess it doesn't really matter. I think our souls are ageless.

My three-year old son knows more than I do now. Sometimes, I ask his advice or guidance. And sometimes, I think he gives it.

The little boy next door will only eat hard-boiled eggs. For it was Easter-time when Christian died. As other children were nibbling the ears off of chocolate bunnies, my son lay dying. Brandon believes if he can "bring back Easter (he can) bring back Christian." He worries, too, because Christian doesn't have his water-gun in Heaven.

Brandon's older sister Danielle understands more. She carries his picture next to her heart, along with pictures of Truffles, her dead cat, and her old house. Sometimes her mom hears her crying at night.

Mallory, Christian's girlfriend on the corner, is concerned because she pushed him. Last week, she pushed Anneka, too, and so worried that Anneka would die.

Ah, the wisdom of children. I told the children that Christian's grandfather's father was with him, teaching him all that he needed to know to be an angel. They liked that. And then I told them they would probably never know another child to die—and I pray they won't. Most children, I reassured, grow up and become mommies and daddies, then grandmas and grandpas. And they ooh'ed and aah'ed at the thought of their own old age.

I sat in his room today and reflected on the half-erased picture on the chalkboard. I tried to discern what he had intended the tangle of chalk ribbons to be. I guessed the "Starship Enterprise", his latest favorite artistic subject—though only a mother could interpret it as such. And I smiled.

It surprises people—even myself—how easy laughter came after his death. Oh, we mourn, and we cry. But we also laugh and remember. And it feels good to remember. I dread the day people stop remembering Christian out loud.

The week he died was the first warm week of the year. The neighbors kept their children indoors in deference. It felt unnatural. We told them so and the children came out to play. The same week, the forsythia bloomed—and so did the daffodils, and, even, the magnolia tree we planted when he was born.

If a child has to die, spring is a good time for his death. Because there is so much new life, we can't help but be joyful, and rejuvenated, and hopeful.

At times like this, many people turn away from God. But strangely, I feel closer to Him. Who better to understand my pain and grief and joy than Him? In some small way, if it's not too arrogant or blasphemous to say, I feel like a kindred spirit to Him. He gave His Son up for me some millennia ago, and so too I gave mine up to him.

Life is good. And so, in its own way, is death.
VWV May 18, 1993

Ramblings of a Bereft Mother

The following excerpt was written a little later in that same year, when I was pregnant with Katrina. I include it here because to understand my grief, you need to understand where I was emotionally that first year.

My husband bent over the body of our beautiful three-year-old, clad so carefully by the hospital personnel in a mint green gown with a grinning Mickey Mouse. (His own clothes cut off in haste, left to mildew in a plastic bag nearby.) "But people don't die from the flu!!" he sobbed—blood-curdling, face-contorting, shoulder-shaking, soul-wrenching sobs. And he was right, as we would find out (later)—at least in Christian James' case.

Strangely, I felt relieved when the Medical Examiner gave a cause of death. At least I had not caused my own child's death, and the guilt was gone. I could finally remember his beautiful face without seeing the sunken eyes and blue lips that had plagued his memory until then.

I didn't even have the benefit of knowing his heart would beat in another child's chest, or that his ocean-colored eyes would help another to watch a sunrise, or that another child would take life-giving breaths with Christian's lungs, saving another parent the agony of losing a child. Because the cause of death was undetermined until the next day, the only body part we could donate was his eyes for research. Perhaps a young doctor somewhere will discover a cure for blindness from Christian's eyes.

Christian was all that a child is. He wasn't perfect. He was willful and stubborn. He threw temper tantrums, and fought with his sister. He did things he knew he wasn't allowed to; he got into things he wasn't supposed to—and he ran wild.

But he was also mischievous and curious, and loving, and affectionate, and sweet and genuine—and all things that are a child.

His father says we are starting our family over—he and I and our younger child, Anneka. It's never been the three of us.

For he was the child who made me a parent—and my parents grandparents. He was the child who first called me "Mommy", the first child to suckle at my breast, and the first to die.

After he died, I used to say, "I have an angel in Heaven and one on Earth." But now I am expecting again, and my children represent Past, Present, and Future. I suppose that's indicative of the circle of life.

A "bittersweetness" comes with this new baby. Two siblings, two lifetimes. Two generations born to the same family. No common bond, no shared experiences, no collective memories. Not even a family picture with all my children's faces. Bridged only by the sister born between them and the parents who birthed them both.

If there is any truth to the birth order theory, then Anneka will succeed in life. Having been the youngest child, an only child, and the oldest child, she should reap the benefits of each. She was not conceived to be the oldest child, or even an only child, and yet…

Strangers ask how many children I have—they see Anneka and assume she is an only child. How do I respond? There is no easy answer. Other family members have begun omitting him from the count. I can't. I still number Christian among my children. When I close my eyes and I picture my children, I see Christian, Anneka, and this new baby.

Worse, strangers and, even, friends don't realize I've already been through the Terrible Two's and potty-training and all the other aspects of raising a toddler.

So, too often I make people uneasy by remembering Christian to them.

I want my surviving children to know their brother—even if they were born after he lived. And so I will tell them of the brother they never knew, and they will grow up too comfortable in cemeteries.

*His name will probably come up daily until my last child passes his oldest age. It's always lowered a half-decibel in reverence when spoken, lest it sounds too loudly. Strangers, acquaintances, even close friends avoid using it altogether—as if speaking it will smite them the same misfortune, or, perhaps, more compassionately, so as not to "remind" us of his death, or of the son we had. As if we **could** forget…*

Of all, though, the hardest thing to endure is giving up my responsibility for him. Anneka asked one night if "She-shinn night-night?" And I didn't know how to answer. I don't know if he sleeps, or needs to; if he's eating, or needs to; or, for that matter, if he's doing what he's supposed to, or what it is he's supposed to be doing. I will always be Christian's Mommy, but I no longer get to "mommy" him.

We raise our children to leave us, prepare them to be on their own— but we don't expect it to happen in three years.

A complete lifetime in three years and twenty days. One-thousand, one-hundred sixteen days. Twenty-six thousand, seven hundred seventy-eight hours, give or take. Middle age at eighteen months. A lifetime in brevity.

I stood in church the other day, remembering a tiny gray casket draped in tulips and lilies—not quite as big as a grocery cart—and the huge pipe organ groaning "You Are My Sunshine" as the funeral dirge, and I wept silently.

I found a toy dinosaur—a tiny, rubber, pink and orange something-o-saurus—deep in the crevices of the couch. No telling how long it had been there. Did a dying tow-headed cherub tuck it in there for his grieving mother to find, months after his death? Or sadder, maybe it was just coincidental that his sister had lost it in its "cave", under the cushions only last week? I will never know.

Sometimes I find loose strands of his hair sticking out of a blanket or pillow. I always replace them after I'm done caressing them—so that I may rediscover them at a later date. I have enough of his hair safely put away. When I visited his lifeless body in the ER, I actually had the presence of mind to request a pair of scissors, to cut a lock of hair. It was the only part of Christian that I could take with me (though, in truth, I did look at his toenails and wonder if I should cut them, too). Just the week before I had given him a haircut. Had I known, I would have saved every strand. Someday, I fear, there will be no mementos of his left to find. As if a celebrity had touched it, I find myself stroking things, saying, "Christian wore this or played with that."

I can't say I am totally used to his absence, this person I was—no, am—so familiar with. If by some miracle, Christian were to walk in the front door tomorrow I could pick up parenting him where I left off. Or could I?

But we have gone on with our lives, and after an awkward transition, adopted new routines.

It's hardest when something changes. It took me weeks to buy new baby shampoo. I milked the bottle for as long as possible. I dreaded buying a new bottle—because **this** *was the shampoo that had washed Christian's hair; he would never have his hair washed with the new shampoo. Somehow, that represented the finality of his death.*

It was the same with the month of May. I hated seeing May come to an end, because it was the first month, whole month, that Christian wasn't alive for at all. And the same with the end of summer, the first full season without him.

A part of me cringes every time we make a new purchase or a change to the house. I think to myself, "Christian never saw this and never will." And there is even a part of me that irrationally fears that if he ever were to return, he wouldn't recognize his home.

But I can't live in a mausoleum. And so children play in his room when they visit. Those who knew him revere in it. And as much as I hated to allow it, overnight guests have slept in there (though some have opted to sleep on our uncomfortable couch rather than disturb the sanctity of his room).

Along the same lines, I don't buy oranges or fruit-roll-ups anymore. Those were two of his favorite snacks and I haven't been able to buy them again, yet.

Sometimes, I feel like Christian and I are still tethered by some invisible umbilicus. I still feel tied to him. There are days I am exuberant for no apparent reason, and I give Christian credit for those days. I know that he's going through something wonderful that he's allowing me to experience a tiny bit. And on really bad days, I remind myself that it must sadden Christian to feel me down. Probably only another mother who has lost a child could relate to the experience; but I assure you, it is very real.

My mother—and even some of my friends—fears I am suicidal because I am "handling things too well." My words are closely metered and if I make mention of death, particularly my own or any beauty I see in the after-life, I am quickly scolded, berated, warned, lectured, and advised against doing anything like "THAT". Oddly, it would make most people more comfortable to see me be inconsolably distraught. But I am confident that I am doing a pretty fair job of coping (as is my husband, Larry). Some people have said that I've inspired them, others that I am repressing. Neither is my intention. I am just trying to get through this thing called grief, and still maintain my sanity. I am dealing in the only way that seems natural to me, yet it amazes me how few people can accept that.

The Will to Survive is a lot stronger than any of us realize. Like any other parent, I had always believed that if something ever happened to one of my children, I'd give up on life. But when he died, I had another child to take care of, and a husband who needed me. And besides, whatever my purpose here is, I haven't completed it yet.

After all, what's sixty or seventy years when you're talking eternity? Still, I can see how some grieving parents could consider suicide an option.

How do I explain grief to someone who has never lost a child? Grief was a stranger to me, before I lost Christian. Now, my constant companion.

It was a new emotion for me. And our language does not distinguish grief by whom we're mourning; there is no word to convey the depth of a parent's grief.

The death of the person—that's bearable, in and of itself. It is not (just) Christian I miss; it's his hugs and kisses and smell and voice and laugh I ache for.

I search the darkness for some hint of him. Maybe in the shadows I can pretend I see him.

I search the faces of strangers' children for his. I never see it.

I search the silence, strain to hear the faint echo of his laughter and words. There's only deafness.

*Once someone has grieved, they have lost forever the luxury of naivete, the leisure of security, the bliss of ignorance. Those "other people" that bad things happen to—well, just don't be too sure they are **other** people. None of us are exempt.*

I did not realize the effect his death would have on others. Frankly, I had never considered it from anyone else's standpoint. Larry and I watched in amazement as our parents and siblings and friends hurt right along with us. One of Christian's grandfathers regretted that he would never take Christian to Disney World; the other that he would never teach him to play baseball.

Christian is outlived by not only his parents, but all of his grandparents and four of his great-grandparents. Ironically, he met my (deceased) grandfather who died before my birth before I will.

Born to immigrant parents, Larry was the first one in his family born in this country. Now, his only son is the first to be buried on American soil. Middletown was just suppose to be a town we settled into after college—not where we would bury our children.

My grief, it has aged me. Not yet out of my twenties, I've already buried a child. How I feel for the pioneer women who buried more children than they raised!

If it accomplishes nothing else, the death of a child certainly puts things into perspective. As I was praying that he would recover, I realized how many trivial prayers I had said—"Please God, let me make this green light", "Please God, let me pass this test!", "Please God, let me win the lottery and I'll never ask for anything else as long as I live!" Somehow, they just didn't stand up to "Please God, don't take this child from me!"

Funny though, looking back, I never bargained with God. I don't regret it, I just find it curious.

*Someone asked me recently (with no malice intended) if his death made me feel like an inadequate parent. It was the kind of question that left **me** with questions. Of course not, but why not? I suppose it's because in our case, Christian's death was a natural one. Had he died, say, by accident or choking or drowning, then maybe I would have felt that way. It made all the difference to me knowing that I—and everyone else—did everything humanly possible to save him.*

In this sue-happy society of ours, Larry and I are constantly defending our decision NOT to sue. It seems odd to have to defend that which we know to be so apparently "right". We still see the same family doctor—much to the surprise of even the doctor. Yet we are constantly bombarded with conversations that start like: "Maybe if the doctor had…"; "You could feel differently in a year—you know you have seven years before the Statutes of Limitations run out…"; "You could donate all the money to charity, if you feel it would taint his memory…"; "Nothing will ever change until you sue…"; "Don't you wonder how many other mistakes the hospital has made…"; "You have got an open and shut case, what have you got to lose…", ad nauseam.

But you can't sue God, and ultimately it was His decision to take my little boy.

Another mail-order catalog arrived the other day. As usual, I dog-eared the pages with potential purchases. Only after I had done so did I realize that I had absent-mindedly marked a page with a toy on it for Christian. "Christian would like this," I thought and turned down the corner. A debilitating sadness came over me when I realized what I had done. I will probably spend and entire lifetime—my own—selecting would-be outfits and toys for him.

In the department store, I look at the little boy clothes. I wonder which winter coat he would have chosen. I can almost picture him in one and I know that's the one.

I will never pick out another Halloween costume for him or buy him a Christmas present or make him an Easter basket. Instead, I will decorate his grave appropriately and hope that suffices.

It was supposed to be his first day of nursery school recently. And as I watched my neighbor prepare her three-year-old for the big day, I wondered if I would get the same ache on his first day of kindergarten, high school, even college. In twenty years, will I pick out some nice young lady and think, "Yes, she would be my daughter-in-law"? I don't know.

I think about his wife and the children they would have had. She, his past-potential bride, is still a child herself. But I wonder if she'll spend a lifetime wandering the world aimlessly, searching for that special someone she was supposed to spend her life with, now a life filled with desperation and loneliness, grieving for the husband she'll never know, who died at age three, and for the children they'll never have.

I envy other parents of angelic-looking little children. I wonder how they got their sons past the dreaded age of three years and twenty days. I know it's foolish, even futile, to question it.

Rainy Mondays are the worst. I always wonder who the parents are who are losing their child that day. My husband reminded me that God doesn't take children only on Mondays—or rainy days. Still there is something ominous and grim about hearing an ambulance siren on a rainy Monday afternoon.

A child's autopsy must be the most gruesome reading material available. In those sixteen pages, I learned more about my child than I ever cared to know.

As I read Christian's, I couldn't help remembering a frog in my junior high biology class I named "Rhonda Pippins". After (dissecting her), I became so attached to Rhonda that I brought her home to keep—until my mother smelled formaldehyde in the dining room. There ended my close association with Rhonda (as well as my liberties for a while, if I recall correctly).

And then came the gruesome image of my naked three year-old laying on a coroner's slab with his belly pinned back, like a biology class frog.

I used to think professionals like coroners, doctors, paramedics, and even, policemen must develop a professional callousness to combat the attachment to those they minister. Since his death, I've been enlightened. Only recently did I learn that the first police officer at my house on that fateful day—who had tried so valiantly to resuscitate Christian—leaned against my house and sobbed after the ambulance pulled away.

*Three-year-olds don't die everyday—at least, not in **my** neighborhood. This could have been anyone's child. Everyone has some child they are close to. The paramedics trembled. The nurses cried. Even the police and doctors were shaken.*

I will never forget the eerie silence in the Emergency Room when my husband and I walked down the corridor after saying goodbye. Every person stopped what they were doing. Our eyes didn't meet any of theirs, but still I was aware of the pity in their faces; their gazes burning into us as we passed them.

In retrospect, Christian must have known he would die young. For at least a year before he died, he refused to say the words "If I should die" when saying his nightly prayers. He would recite the entire prayer, starting with "Now I lay me down to sleep...", without hesitation until those words. After coaxing him five or six times, he would finally say them, then continue unassisted with the rest of the prayer.

Months before his death, he watch the movie "My Girl", which very discreetly presents the death of a young boy. Christian immediately understood the significance of the boy's glasses falling to the ground and screamed inconsolably until we turned the movie off. A week later, his father's glasses fell off in a store and, once again, he was inconsolable, screaming, "His glasses dropped! His glasses dropped!"

Literally overnight, about a month before his death, he became a much sweeter child. He no longer needed to sit time-out. He showed incredible concern for his sister and others' well being. He got upset a lot less. I attributed the change, at the time, to his outgrowing the Terrible Two's, since his third birthday was nearing. But I think now, he must have sensed what was coming.

And so I witnessed the making of an angel, right before my eyes. And in some way, I played a small part in preparing him for that role.

I know I've been blessed. I've also gone through the Hell of losing a child—my first-born. But if it meant never knowing Christian James Vanderveen and never experiencing his death, I would gladly relive it a thousand times, just to have known him, however briefly.

For it would have been a far emptier life of mine had I never been blessed with his company for three glorious years and twenty days. And sadder still, I would not have known it.

A Mother Knows

Sweet smells
that burn the nostrils still
      and tastes that linger yet.

Memories
held to the breast
      closer than child who dwelt.

Angels sang
a sweet refrain,
      and then he slipped away.

Too dear, too sweet
for life itself,
      I held him in repose.

And knowing what
a mother does,
      I gave him peace to go.

VWV

Most parents I have met who have lost children, say they knew they would lose a child. And in retrospect, they describe the lost children with a radiance, a quality they can not define but that somehow emanates from the soul of their child.

Christian was like that. Strangers would watch him, wherever we went, with a kind of far-off look. Perhaps, they recognized an earth-bound angel. Or perhaps, it was part of his destiny to touch even strangers while he was here.

There is so much I would like to tell you about *how* I knew Christian would die young—but I can not find the words. Suffice it to say, a mother knows.

MARY, MOTHER OF JESUS

Angels on high, in heaven above
Is your song a little richer now?
A child has joined your choir
        to sweeten your music
        as he did our lives
Feathered wings
        to adorn his back
        where
        a vinyl raincoat used to
Golden halo
        rings
        his already glowing towhead
        where
        a cowboy hat once sat
Mary,
Mother of the Most Righteous,
        opens
        her lap to him
        as I did
And Father of Fathers
        cradles him in His embrace
        like his own
        father once had
Countenance so bright
        this child's of mine,

Perhaps I had
       something to do with
       the making of this angel
For it would have been a
       far emptier life of mine
       had he not been in it,
          however so brief
And sadder still,
       I would not have
       known it.

Sometimes, I think of Mary, mother of the holiest child, Jesus Christ. She was the first Christian. But this was her baby—the child who suckled at her breast, the child who made her a mother—up there on the cross. If she knew all that was in store for her child when she agreed to conceive him, would she still have agreed to it? *Would I have?*

I am a flawed human being. I am not purporting to be as righteous or as pious as Mary was. But I have an idea of the pain she must have felt watching her son die. She had thirty-three years with her son; I had three, but had it been thirty-three it still would not have been long enough. If it had been one-hundred and three, it would not even have been long enough.

He would not have been the Jesus Christ he was, had it not been for Mary. And, I suppose, Christian James, would not have been the sweet, lovable, mischievous child that he was had it not been for the parents he was born to.

Someone far wiser than me once wrote that, "'Tis better to have loved than lost, than never to have loved at all." If I knew then what I know now, would I have still had Christian? Absolutely.

ANNELIES

You start life
        amidst bells and whistles,
        tubes and wires—
                not the birth experience I
                expected for you.

Your cry is like the kitten's
        that tried to roar—
        and with that robust "mew"
                you let us know you are
                in our lives for good.

Even now,
        strangers scurry around
                you with competency,
                taking care of your every need.
                        But they are not me.
And as much as I appreciate
        the blessings of modern medicine—
                I see the irony.

Then, there is the moment I
        hold you, finally.
Days old,
        you grab onto my finger,

look me directly in the eye,
and coo to me your life story.
Where have I been,
you must wonder.
I have been with you,
dear child,
and a million miles away.

In sympathy,
my own chest aches
when I watch yours heave.
What I would do to
take your pain, if only I could.

But you have learned
Lesson Number One in Life
too early:
Some things you have to go
through alone.

Here's Lesson Number Two:
Mommy is here for you,
no matter what.

I applaud your milestones
that I took for granted
with your siblings.
You are already a
Lesson in Patience for me.

Lesson Number Three:
You're never too old to learn a thing

or two from someone else.
You are my teacher,
    and I am yours.

So, Sweet Annelies,
    the one who roars like a kitten,
      be prepared for
        the education of a lifetime.

And remember,
    Lesson Number Four:
      Disregard Lesson Number One,
      You are never alone,
        No matter how it may feel.

    I love you,
    Mommy.

    VWV June 1998

Sweet, innocent Annelies,

Your birth was an excruciating lesson in Patience. The Benevolent God of ours realized I had much to learn about tragedy, and gave you pneumonia at birth—five weeks earlier than expected. And so again I was reminded my surviving children are not immortal just because one was sacrificed.

The night you were born, you were whisked away before I had a chance to hold you. Later, I could not even touch you because the contact made you agitated. And so my tears fell on your naked skin as I prayed for your recovery.

When they whisked you away after your delivery, the doctor prepared us for the worst. "She's not breathing right. We may have to transfer her to another hospital, one that has a more advanced NICU." And in the back of my mind all I could think was, "Not *my* child. Obviously you don't know how strong *my* children are."

Later, the nurse came in and asked if we were Christians. Yes, I said. "Then, do you want me to call a clergy person to come in to baptize your baby?"

Never had anyone asked that with any of my four previous babies. I now realized the severity of the situation. But even still, there was a cockiness that God wouldn't *dare* take another one of my children. I declined, and you were baptized in our own church four weeks later, in the gown your father and sisters wore.

But for eight days, your home was an incubator a half-hour from our house. We taped photographs and hand-drawn pictures from your sisters on the plexi-glass, next to the list of emergency instructions. I had to garner a miraculous recovery to go home myself, but thirty-eight hours after your C-section, I was wheeled out of the hospital, empty-handed except for a few "It's A Girl!" balloons and a suitcase.

I would spend all day in the NICU with you, even when I could not hold you. Your roommates were one and two pound babies, no bigger than kittens themselves. The doctors would walk by your incubator and say, "My, what a big baby!" You were all of five pounds. And more than one person commented how you had the face of a cherub.

I talked to you and to your brother constantly during those days. I talk to him everyday anyway, because I figure *his* prayers have to reach the Big Guy a little sooner than mine. I know he was close to you then.

And now, at fifteen months, you are an energetic, healthy little spitfire, no worse for wear. But I am.

I am older now, more jaded. I know how precious life is, and I know our family is not immune from crises. I don't ask God anymore, "How much more? Haven't we been through enough?"—because there is a reason for all things. I take things as they come now. And I know I am strong enough to handle anything, as long as it is temporary. And all things are temporary.

You are my baby—in all likelihood, the last one I will have. I can't imagine not having you—or any of your siblings, for that matter.

I am in awe when you display some of your brother's mannerisms. You are the one farthest removed from him. How will your life be affected by a brother who died so long before you were born?

Since your birth, we have moved from the house where he lived. You will have no memories of his home on Earth. But in the yard, there are five flowering trees planted. Each a different variety, each planted when my children were born. Yours is still a sapling. But it will grow tall and strong, like you. And it will provide beauty in the spring and comfort in the summer, and it will give back to the earth its leaves in the autumn. Just like you.

FANTASIES

Occasionally—very, very rarely—I allow myself to fantasize that Christian returns to us. It is not a fantasy that I give into very often. But on those infrequent, unbearable days, I give myself permission to imagine Christian growing up with his four sisters.

I look for his face in the faces of boys his age. Every so often I pick out clothes for him, even now. I walk by the boys' department and guess what size he would wear and what styles he would prefer. Sometimes I can see him in my mind wearing something and I know that's it. Every Halloween I choose a costume for him, and every winter I choose a coat for him, and every Christmas I choose presents for him—presents he will never open and I will never purchase.

In my mind he is tall, with shorter hair. He is nine now. And he moves with the grace of a younger version of your father. He is compassionate and kind, serious, yet upbeat. He still has that mischievous twinkle in his eye that he did when he was a baby. He plays sports, I imagine. Probably soccer. Maybe baseball, too. *Which team would be his favorite?* Maybe, the Braves, like his father. Or the Sox, like me. Or maybe, the Angels, because for a short time he was an earth-bound angel in our care.

I watch his former playmates grow up, using their milestones as yardsticks in what would be his development. The mothers of other nine-year-olds don't realize how much I take from their children. I *absorb* their childhood, into Christian's memory. *How tall would he be? What would his voice be like now? What fads would he follow? Which teachers would he have—and which subjects would he excel at? What lessons would he have learned had he stayed here until manhood? And what more would he have taught me?*

I allow myself these fantasies—occasionally. But fantasies don't last and they are not tangible. Too well I know, they are only fantasies, and I must return to reality.

DREAMS

Dreams are a beautiful escape. But one of the things that caught me off-guard after Christian died was how infrequently I would dream of him. I had always dreamt of my children, so why now that he was dead couldn't I? I could not even be with him in my dreams when I wanted to. Not only had I lost the dreams I had had *for* him, now I had lost the dreams I had *of* him.

But finally he came to me in a dream. And I woke up elated that I had been in his presence. That is exactly how it felt—that I had been with Christian. And his hugs were still fresh and his scent was somehow near. But later, I sank into a deep depression; the post-dream adrenaline wearing off. I would soon discover this would be the pattern following "Christian dreams".

Overall, in the past six years, I have probably only had a couple dozen dreams with Christian in them, if that many. Sadder, your father rarely remembers his dreams; so even the ones he has had, he can't remember. I believe he can count the number of dreams he has had on one hand. I am more fortunate.

A couple of years after he died, just prior to Mother's Day, I began finding four-leaf clovers everywhere—even at the corner of Christian's headstone. Some people have never found a four-leaf clover, but in my life I have found many—a benefit of my Irish heritage, I suppose. But that particular week I found 13.

Then, Mother's Day night I had a dream about Christian. We talked, in the dream, about inconsequential stuff. But then as the dream started to come to a close and he was drifting farther and farther away, all of a sudden he came close to me. He held his fist out. When he turned it over, I could see his fingernails so clearly. He slowly uncurled his fist and inside were crumpled clovers—a few of the flowers and some of the four-leave variety. And he said these words to me, "Some mother's get roses on Mother's Day, but I send you clovers." With that he dropped the handful into my own hand and the dream ended.

I woke up clutching my hand so tightly, my fingernails left marks in my palm. I slowly uncurled my fingers, sure there would be clovers in my hand. When there weren't, I franticly searched the sheets and bedding. The realization that it was just a dream dropped over me like a pall. But I opened my journal to record the dream anyway, and there, on the next blank page was a perfectly pressed four-leaf clover. (And no, I don't remember placing it there.)

Since then, every four-leaf clover I have found, I know that it is Christian sending it to me—and around Mother's Day every year since, I always find several, though the number varies from year to year.

People always ask me how old Christian is when he comes to me in a dream. He is usually his appropriate age. He is no longer three.

When he was five, I had another significant dream. In it, I saw him at five, and he showed me the baby teeth he had lost and how straight the new ones were coming in. I told him his friend across the street had just lost her first tooth too, and he replied, "I know."

Later, in the same dream, I saw him as a young man. I relish that image. He was about nineteen or twenty, I would guess. He was physically fit and he had some of your father's mannerisms. He stretched and it was like seeing your father at nineteen. His blond hair was longish, but neat. It was all one length and he pulled it into a ponytail in his fist, with the ease someone who is used to having long hair mindlessly plays with their hair. But his face was all Christian. There was no denying who he was. He was so handsome and strong and confident and mature. I know I have seen my son as an adult.

SPIRITUAL

I will never be a prophet,
But I have…
> *Seen angels*
> *and reveled in the splendor of dandelions*
> *and heard my children laugh in their sleep*
> *and been alone with God, in my own little world.*

I have witnessed miracles,
> *that defy reason*
> *and heard the Song of Nature.*

I have climbed mountains
> *and have fallen down*
> *and climbed up again.*

VWV

These are the hardest words to write. My spiritual experiences are the most personal part of my being, but I will share them with you, finally. I do not discuss them with many people—they are private, they are *mine*, they are all true, and they are a huge part of who I am. So take a deep breath, because once you read what I have to say, you will never look at your mother the same way again.

I collect angels, and I am sure you probably think that is because your brother is an angel now. That is not the only reason.

I surround myself with them physically, as well as spiritually. I call for their protection in the car or when I am alone. I "send" them to friends in need. I thank them for the little unexpected surprises that happen over the course of the day. I ask them to watch over you children when I can not (and often, when I can).

Have I seen angels? Yes, I have. Both winged and wingless. Am I special for having seen them? No, just more open to them. The Bible tells us we will entertain angels unawares; I have just been fortunate enough to recognize a few of mine.

I have watched angels kneel over you, my children, and hover nearby, and escort you down staircases. I have seen angels stand over your father as he sleeps, arms outstretched. I have seen them at the corners of my bed, and in my living room. There have been more than I can relate here—and some too personal to relate. But here are a few incidences I think are important enough to include.

Once, as I watched helplessly, a car veered into the lane of the car which carried one of you girls and your father. (I was driving the car behind your father's car.) An angel stood through your father's car, with uplifted wings, and made a *bubble* around the entire car. The second car bounced off the blue bubble and back into its own lane.

Another time, I heard, very loudly, very specifically, "There will be an accident", as I left the airport, having dropped off your grandmother for a flight. I said a quick prayer—for her safety as well as my own. Minutes later, I was behind two tractor-trailer trucks. I could not pass either one, no matter how hard I tried to accelerate. I acquiesced, and returned to the spot behind the trucks. Suddenly, all traffic stopped. My view of what happened blocked by the trucks. When traffic resumed a few minutes later, I discovered there *had* been an accident—right in front of the truck in front of me. Had I passed it, I would have been sandwiched between the two semis.

I watched as a six -winged angel descended from the ceiling at Christian's funeral. He was tall—or rather, long. He wrapped first one pair of wings around his face; then, a second pair around his feet. And the third, largest, pair around his torso, completing a cocoon, of sorts, around himself. It is the only time I have seen a six-winged angel.

And then there is the Lady. I have no name for her, so I call her the Lady with the Lyrical Voice. When she first began coming to me, it was just as a voice—a voice so familiar to me, so recognizable it was like hearing my own mother's voice. Then, she would come to me in a cloud—usually just to the left of me, and above—still with the same sweet, lyrical voice. Always accompanied by a beautiful aroma of flowers—roses and lilacs, and other unidentifiable floral scents.

The first time I saw her was a few days after Christmas, when Christian was not yet two. Your father was downstairs reading. The clock read somewhere around 12:30 a.m. Christian slept in our bed next to me, having developed the sniffles and wheezing, just before bedtime. I groggily woke to hear him talking his baby-talk in his sleep. It was gibberish, but whomever he was speaking to, understood what he was saying and was responding to him the same way. (*Do babies actually speak in the Tongues of Angels?*). I opened my eyes, and rolled over to see a woman leaning over Christian. I can not tell you if she was fifteen, or forty-five, but she seemed young. Over her shoulders and head, she wore several scarves—all varying shades of blue, except one crimson scarf. She was as tangible and flesh as I am.

I turned back over. Then it hit me, and I looked back at them, and the Lady was still there. She said, "You've got to take care of that or it will get worse," (the sniffles, I presume). I said I would. Then, I jumped out of bed. She must have realized I panicked, because she pulled the red scarf over her face and went over to the wall, by the armoire. Your brave mother ran out of the room.

Larry called up, "Are you all right?" I said I was, then realized I had left Christian alone with this woman. When I went back, she was gone. I have always wished that I had kept my composure so I could have talked to her more. But angelic visits are not an everyday occurrence—even for me.

I followed her advice, and put menthol-rub on Christian's chest, and he was better by morning.

I had a few more experiences, but none as *awesome* as that one, until March 12, 1993—one month exactly before Christian's death. The following morning, this is what I wrote verbatim in my journal:

> *March 13, 1993*
> *The Lady with the Lyrical Voice came back! With a big white horse. The horse was unbridled and bareback. She stood to its right. We spoke but I don't remember the conversation. Seems it involved a journey— going somewhere with them or having just returned. Anneka woke up and I had to feed her. Even as I was feeding her, I was groggily aware of someone in the room (by Larry's bureau). After, when I was lying in bed trying to evaluate it, I could almost feel the softness of her scarves. I think she wears harem pants—very billowy, out of a lightweight scarf- like material. I hope she comes back. I trust her!*

She spoke about a transition and a metamorphosis. I honestly thought she was warning me of my own death. I knew the horse had something to do with death. It did not occur to me that it was my child's. The horse whinnied and pawed at the carpet as the Lady and I spoke. While I fed Anneka, I would not look at the Lady or the horse any longer. In my peripheral vision, I could see them for a few more minutes. Then they went away. But before they left, I felt something brush my cheek—*her scarf, a kiss?* I am not sure.

In the morning, I told Larry and my mother of the experience, lest it was my own death she was foreshadowing. They both dismissed it, but a month later, we all understood it was Christian's death she was talking about, not mine.

But oddest of all, when I checked the carpet the day after their visit, there were three deep, round circle-marks in the plush carpet, forming a large, right triangle. Where a fourth hoof would be, the carpet was scuffed up.

The Lady came back to me, after Christian died, too. I could feel her with me at the hospital. I was almost certain that if I put my hand on my shoulder, I would feel her hand resting there.

Two days after his death—the afternoon of his viewing—I laid down to try to get some much-needed rest. I was not yet asleep when I sensed someone in the room with me. I looked up, and in broad daylight, there was my friend, the Lady With the Lyrical Voice. This time, without the horse.

"Christian. Where is Christian?" I asked. And without a word, she lifted her arm, and with a sweeping motion (à la game show hostess opening a curtain), the walls became the sky and I saw *Jesus* walking with Christian. They were both all blue, even their skin—the color of the sky. Jesus looked right at me—he was so tall, next to my boy. Then, they took hands; both waved, and turned and walked away. I settled back onto my pillow, content. And for the first time in days, I felt like I could breathe.

She has returned a few times since—each time I am wide awake, or, at least, in between sleep and wakefulness—though never with the same intensity. I know I will see her again. I do not know who she is to me—*a guardian angel, an ancestor*? I do not presume she is Mary, mother of Jesus, but others have suggested it to me. Until she tells me otherwise, she is the Lady with the Lyrical Voice— and my friend.

I have often wondered if it was she who accompanied Christian to Heaven. There are a thousand questions I would love to ask her. But when she comes to me, she usually seems to be there for a reason, and, awestruck, I lose my presence of mind to ask her to stay and chat.

MEMORIALS

She worked the clay
and with muddied hands
formed
the image
of a boy
she never met

And the clay remembered,
and obliged
a mother's prayer

And the sculptress
found
in a lump of
terra cotta
the spirit
of a boy she never met.

For Wynne White
VWV 1994

Probably the two things I would save if my house was on fire and everyone was safe would be the terra cotta sculpture of Christian and his quilt.

When I got the idea to commission a sculpture, it was like a light bulb had gone off. It seemed so unrealistic, though. So I prayed about it—really, really prayed on it. And the answer I kept getting was, "You'll know by the name." It made no sense, but I trusted. So, I called an art studio affiliated with a local liberal arts college. The only sculpture's name they could give me was that of a local woman by the name of Wynne White—and then I knew. My middle name is Wynne (Anneka's middle name is also Wynne) and I had never met another Wynne, so she was it. It still amazes me that she was able to capture the essence of Christian in a lump of mud and she never knew him.

From almost immediately after his death, I knew I wanted to make a quilt with his clothing, but it took almost two-and-a-half years until I was emotionally ready to do it. I knew that if I ever had another son, I would not be able to dress him in some of Christian's outfits. Try as I might, giving them away was impossible. Oddly, his baby clothes did not affect me like that—probably because I considered them *my babies'* clothes. Anneka had worn many of them, and later the rest of you girls would, too. But the clothes in his drawers and closets when he died seemed sacred. So I lovingly cut them into squares and pieced them into a priceless quilt, bordered by a sunshiny-yellow blanket-ribbon. Every square tells a story. From the paint-stained T-shirt to his favorite pajamas to the shirt the ER doctors cut off of him. In the middle: his name trimmed from a sweatshirt that was a gift from your Beppe. Hugging that quilt is like hugging him, sometimes. And stroking the patches, I can remember his *feel.* It lies at the foot of my bed twelve months a year.

There is a pair of blue pajamas I chose not to include, however. You see, there are still a few strands of his hair on that pair. I reserve hugging those until I really, REALLY need to feel him.

There are songs I listen to when I need a good cry—because, sometimes, there is nothing as cleansing as a good cry. And other songs I listen to when I need a pick-me-up—because I have learned the hard way that you can't cry while you're bee-bopping around the kitchen.

The week after he died, Larry and I treated ourselves to necklaces to memorialize him. On your dad's—a thick heavy gold cross—are the letters "CJV" going down and the date "4-12-93" (his death date) going across. Mine is a tiny locket with a cross on the front and on the back "CJV 3-23-90 to 4-12-93". Inside is his picture.

A tiny silver box sits on my dresser, a gold angel perched on top. Inside the box is a coil of golden hair—a lock I snipped off in the ER after he died. Incredibly, I had the presence of mind to ask for a pair of scissors, but I think it scared the hospital staff when I did; they were not sure what I was planning on doing with them.

His raincoat and cowboy hat still hang in our coat closet, with the rest of our coats—because he is still a member of our family. And his likeness graces our walls, alongside photographs of you girls. But alas, there will be no new pictures of Christian, to update our gallery.

COMPASSION

You ask how I do it,
        how I go on.
Are you sure you want to know?
Do you realize it has been four years since he left—
        gone now longer than he was here?

If I am very still sometimes,
        I can feel him in the wind.
                A breeze that kisses my cheek,
                        so tenderly,
                        —and I know it's him.

Do you really want to know
        that sometimes I compare other boys to mine
                —his height, his laugh, his mannerisms?

Occasionally,
        I still shop for boy's clothes
                and Christmas presents
                        —delusions, I am only too aware,
                                are luxuries.

And since you asked—
        I take things slower now.
                I find the glory in a field of clovers

and he is there.

You ask how I do it,
> *I see other parents and*
>> *wonder the same thing.*
I still do not know where
> *his father found the strength*
>> *— but I know it was infectious.*

You ask "Why?"
> *I can't.*
I'm afraid I couldn't handle the answer now.
> *Someday, I will understand.*
> *I take comfort in the blessings I have today.*
That's enough.

I am still his mother,
He is still my son.
> *Others forget.*
> *I won't.*
> *Not ever.*

But of all the mothers in all the universe,
> *he was given to **me**.*
>> *Even briefly,*
>>> *it is more than anyone else had.*

You ask me how I do it—
> *Honestly,*
>> *there weren't a lot of options.*

VWV

When I meet someone who also has lost a child, there is an unspoken empathy. A kind of relief at having met someone who *knows*. As if we are brethren in a secret fraternity, immediately there is a connection. And yet, our brotherhood is far too vast.

My own grandmother has buried four of her five children. I do not want to know this grief again. But if it is God's Will, then I will make the best of it.

Only someone who has been through it can know what it is like to shop for a dress for her son's funeral (the man behind the counter told me to "Have a nice day"—and I stared at him blankly). Or to design a headstone; or wake up in the middle of the night, sure you heard him crying. Only someone who has been through it can know what it is like to follow a child who looks remarkably like your own from the back, just so you can be disappointed by their face when they turn around. Or know the ache when you wake up from a dream about them and realize that is as close to them as you can ever get again. Or know what it feels like to attend a wedding and realize you will never attend your own child's. And only a parent who has lost a child knows what it is like to mark time by "before he died" and "since his death".

If I have learned nothing else from Christian's death, it is to be more compassionate. I know that a little bit of heartfelt compassion goes a long way, and saying the "wrong" thing is infinitely better than saying nothing at all.

Shortly after his death, your father, both sets of grandparents, and I attended a Compassionate Friends meeting. It is a group of bereaved parents who meet to discuss their children among others who understand. I learned so much there that day. The one parent who seemed to have the most reason to be angry (because of the way her child died), seemed to have the most peace. And other parents whose children had been gone several decades seemed to still be in fresh grief. But they knew my pain— *our* pain. And I could see, from them, that no matter how bad it got—and it would—there were days ahead to look forward to.

...AND FINALLY...

My Son, O, my son,
            what did you do today?

            Perhaps, you played starball,
                        or ran around the moon.

            Maybe you made sunshine,
                        or laid on clouds 'til noon.

            Or rather, greeted newcomers
                                    to the Gates of Paradise
                        or drifted on God's breath
                                    to the Universe's heights.

            Whatever that it is,
                        that occupies your days,

            Remember, remember this:
                        though life on Earth is brief,
                                    its effect will ever stay.

                                    VWV January 28, 1994

So children, this is my story. It is unique, it is mine, and, with any luck, it has given you insight into your own childhood.

Writing this for you has been an intense lesson in grief for myself, as well. I have tried to be as candid as possible.

Psychologists will tell you there are x-number of stages of grief and that there is a certain course that it follows. I have found there are infinitely more emotions and stages than can be put down on paper. It is less one emotion than an all-consuming way of life—one in which your father and I live everyday, no hope for remission or recuperation.

One more thing, I want you to realize especially, that if it had only been a matter of faith and prayer, your brother would be alive today. But sometimes, you have to say, "Let Thy will be done," and accept the outcome.

I still count your brother among my children. There are times, when I do a head-count and I have to remind myself he is gone. There are days he feels so close that I swear I can feel him breathe. Other days, he is so distant, it almost feels like it was another lifetime ago that I was his mother.

Today it is another rainy Monday—not unlike the one on which your brother died. But rainy Mondays do not paralyze me anymore like they once did. I can snuggle into the warmth of our home, content in the knowledge all my children are safe.

Down the hall, the Dutch clock of your father's chimes the hour—comforting me, reminding me I am never really alone. From where I sit, I can see the fresh grave of our beloved mutt, Louie, whom we had to put to sleep just last week. As much a member of our family that he was, it was not like burying a child—I have done both. I do not care to repeat either again in my lifetime. But we have other pets, and God willing, I will outlive them. And I also have other children; and sadly, the price of loving you, is taking the risk that I may outlive you, as well. A risk I am willing to take.

Tonight, as you sleep, I will check your beds several times. Reassurance, I suppose. I know I am over-protective. You may hate me when you are an adult for being too cautious, for not allowing certain things, for hovering too much—but at least, you will make it to adulthood.

And late at night, when I am alone with my thoughts, and my body is heavy with fatigue, and my mind drifts between the two worlds where my children live, if I am very lucky, I will feel someone take my hand. Or perhaps, a cool breeze will brush across my cheek. Or sense a presence in the room, so tangible. And I will know that my son is near.

There is so much more to tell you. You are still children and I cannot do it all here. But there comes a point when one more word ruins the story. So I leave you with this:

I will love you forever
Christian,

Anneka,

Katrina,

Liesel,

Annelies.

Peace,
Mom

About the Author

Vicki W. Vanderveen lives in Clifton Park, New York, with her husband and best friend, Larry, and their four beautiful daughters Anneka, Katrina, Liesel, and Annelies, and a menagerie of pets. In her ample spare time, she continues to write and paints.

www.ingramcontent.com/pod-product-compliance
Lightning Source LLC
Chambersburg PA
CBHW020249290526
45784CB00003B/1165